United States Government Accountability

Report to the Chairman,
Homeland Security and Governmer
Affairs, U.S. Senate

May 2014

FEDERAL SOFTWARE LICENSES

Better Management Needed to Achieve Significant Savings Government-Wide

FEDERAL SOFTWARE LICENSES

Better Management Needed to Achieve Significant Savings Government-Wide

GAO Highlights

Highlights of GAO-14-413, a report to the Chairman, Committee on Homeland Security and Governmental Affairs, U.S. Senate

Why GAO Did This Study

The federal government plans to spend at least $82 billion on IT products and services in fiscal year 2014, such as software licenses. Federal agencies engage in thousands of licensing agreements annually. Effective management of software licenses can help avoid purchasing too many licenses that result in unused software.

GAO was asked to review federal agencies' management of software licenses. GAO (1) assessed the extent to which OMB and federal agencies have appropriate policies on software license management, (2) determined the extent to which agencies adequately manage licenses, and (3) described agencies' most widely used software and extent to which they were over or under purchased. GAO assessed policies from 24 agencies and OMB against sound licensing policy measures. GAO also analyzed and compared agencies' software inventories and management controls to leading practices, and interviewed responsible officials. To identify sound licensing policy measures and leading practices, GAO interviewed recognized private sector and government software license management experts.

What GAO Recommends

GAO recommends OMB issue a directive to help guide agencies in managing licenses and that the 24 agencies improve their policies and practices for managing licenses. OMB disagreed with the need for a directive, but GAO believes it is needed, as discussed in the report. Most agencies generally agreed with the recommendations or had no comments.

View GAO-14-413. For more information, contact Carol R. Cha at (202) 512-4456 or chac@gao.gov.

What GAO Found

The Office of Management and Budget (OMB) and the vast majority of agencies that GAO reviewed do not have adequate policies for managing software licenses. While OMB has a policy on a broader information technology (IT) management initiative that is intended to assist agencies in gathering information on their IT investments, including software licenses, it does not guide agencies in developing comprehensive license management policies. Regarding agencies, of the 24 major federal agencies, 2 have comprehensive policies that include the establishment of clear roles and central oversight authority for managing enterprise software license agreements, among other things; 18 have them but they are not comprehensive; and 4 have not developed any. The weaknesses in agencies' policies were due, in part, to the lack of a priority for establishing software license management practices and a lack of direction from OMB. Without an OMB directive and comprehensive policies, it will be difficult for the agencies to consistently and effectively manage software licenses.

Federal agencies are not adequately managing their software licenses because they generally do not follow leading practices in this area. The table lists the leading practices and the number of agencies that have fully, partially, or not implemented them.

24 Major Agencies' Implementation of Software License Management Leading Practices

Leading practice	Fully implemented	Partially implemented	Not implemented
Centralized management	4	15	5
Established software license inventory	2	20	2
Tracking and maintain inventory	0	20	4
Analyzing software license data	0	15	9
Providing sufficient training	0	5	19

Source: GAO analysis of agency data.

The inadequate implementation of leading practices in software license management was partially due to weaknesses in agencies' policies. As a result, agencies' oversight of software license spending is limited or lacking, and they may miss out on savings. The potential savings could be significant considering that, in fiscal year 2012, one major federal agency reported saving approximately $181 million by consolidating its enterprise license agreements even though its oversight process was ad hoc.

Given that agencies lack comprehensive software license inventories that are regularly tracked and maintained, GAO cannot accurately describe the most widely used software applications across the government, including the extent to which they were over and under purchased. Further, the data provided by agencies regarding their most widely used applications had limitations. Specifically, (1) agencies with data provided them in various ways, including by license count, usage, and cost; (2) the data provided by these agencies on the most widely used applications were not always complete; and (3) not all agencies had available data on the most widely used applications. Until weaknesses in how agencies manage licenses are addressed, the most widely used applications cannot be determined and thus opportunities for savings across the federal government may be missed.

_____ **United States Government Accountability Office**

Contents

Tables

Abbreviations

CIO	chief information officer
Commerce	Department of Commerce
Defense	Department of Defense
DHS	Department of Homeland Security
DOT	Department of Transportation
Education	Department of Education
Energy	Department of Energy
EPA	Environmental Protection Agency
GSA	General Services Administration
HHS	Department of Health and Human Services
HUD	Department of Housing and Urban Development
Interior	Department of the Interior
IT	information technology
Justice	Department of Justice
Labor	Department of Labor
NASA	National Aeronautics and Space Administration
NSF	National Science Foundation
NRC	Nuclear Regulatory Commission
OMB	Office of Management and Budget
OPM	Office of Personnel Management
SBA	Small Business Administration
SSA	Social Security Administration
State	Department of State
Treasury	Department of the Treasury
USAID	U.S. Agency for International Development
USDA	Department of Agriculture
VA	Department of Veterans Affairs

May 22, 2014

The Honorable Thomas R. Carper
Chairman
Committee on Homeland Security and Governmental Affairs
United States Senate

Dear Mr. Chairman:

The federal government plans to spend at least $82 billion on information technology (IT) products and services in fiscal year 2014, such as purchases of software licenses.[1] More than 4 million desktop, laptop, and networked computers serve as essential tools for achieving the missions of federal agencies.

Federal agencies engage in thousands of licensing agreements annually. Effective management of software licenses can help organizations avoid purchasing too many licenses that result in unused software. In addition, effective management can help avoid purchasing too few licenses, which results in noncompliance with license terms and causes the imposition of additional fees.

You asked us to review federal agencies' management of software licenses. Our objectives were to (1) assess the extent to which the Office of Management and Budget (OMB) and federal agencies have appropriate policies on software license management, (2) determine the extent to which federal agencies are adequately managing software licenses, and (3) describe the software applications most widely used by the federal agencies and the extent to which they were over or under purchased.

To address our first objective, we identified seven elements that comprehensive software license policies should contain by interviewing six recognized software license management experts from the private and federal sectors and comparing OMB guidance, relevant executive orders, other federal guidance, and professional publications against the

---

[1]According to the Information Technology Infrastructure Library's *Guide to Software Asset Management*, software licenses are legal rights to use software in accordance with terms and conditions specified by the software copyright owner.

elements that had been identified.[2] Further, we analyzed OMB guidance, interviewed OMB staff, and analyzed policies for managing software licenses from the 24 Chief Financial Officers Act agencies[3] against the seven elements for establishing comprehensive policies.

To accomplish the second objective, we identified five leading practices for software license management by interviewing experts and comparing the results to relevant guidance and professional publications, as described for our first objective.[4] For each of the 24 agencies, we compared the agencies' practices with the five leading practices. In addition, we obtained and analyzed relevant software license information such as budget documentation for fiscal years 2012 and 2013, software contracts, and software license inventories for fiscal years 2012 and 2013. We also obtained information through interviews with officials responsible for software license management activities.

Finally, for our third objective, to describe the most widely used software applications, we reviewed and analyzed the agencies' software inventories or agencies' self-reported lists of applications according to volume and spending for each of the 24 major federal agencies. We also interviewed agency officials to determine whether data were available on the extent to which software licenses were over or under purchased for these applications.

We conducted this performance audit from March 2013 to May 2014 in accordance with generally accepted government auditing standards. Those standards require that we plan and perform the audit to obtain sufficient, appropriate evidence to provide a reasonable basis for our findings and conclusions based on our audit objectives. We believe that the evidence obtained provides a reasonable basis for our findings and

---

[2]Please see appendix I for detailed information on our methodology.

[3]The 24 major federal agencies covered by the Chief Financial Officers Act of 1990 are the Departments of Agriculture, Commerce, Defense, Education, Energy, Health and Human Services, Homeland Security, Housing and Urban Development, the Interior, Justice, Labor, State, Transportation, the Treasury, and Veterans Affairs; Environmental Protection Agency; General Services Administration; National Aeronautics and Space Administration; National Science Foundation; Nuclear Regulatory Commission; Office of Personnel Management; Small Business Administration; Social Security Administration; and U.S. Agency for International Development.

[4]Please see appendix I for detailed information on our methodology.

conclusions based on our audit objectives. Additional details of our scope and methodology are contained in appendix I.

Background

OMB and federal agencies have key roles and responsibilities for overseeing IT investment management. OMB is responsible for working with agencies to ensure investments are appropriately planned and justified pursuant to the Clinger-Cohen Act of 1996.[5] The law places responsibility for managing investments with the heads of agencies and establishes chief information officers (CIO) to advise and assist agency heads in carrying out this responsibility.[6] Additionally, this law requires OMB to establish processes to analyze, track, and evaluate the risks and results of major capital investments in information systems made by federal agencies and report to Congress on the net program performance benefits achieved as a result of these investments.

Federal agencies are responsible for managing their IT investment portfolio, including the risks from their major information system initiatives, in order to maximize the value of these investments to the agency. Federal agencies expect to spend at least $82 billion in fiscal year 2014 to meet their increasing demand for IT products and services, such as purchases of software licenses.

Additionally, two executive orders contain information for federal agencies relative to the management of software licenses. In particular, executive order 13103[7] specifies that each agency shall adopt policies and procedures to ensure that the agency uses only computer software not in violation of copyright laws. These procedures may include information on preparing agency software inventories. Additionally, as part of executive order 13589,[8] on promoting efficient spending, agencies are required to assess current device inventories and usage, and establish controls to ensure that they are not paying for unused or underutilized IT equipment, installed software, or services.

---

[5] 40 U.S.C §§ 11302-11303.

[6] 40 U.S.C §§ 11312, 11313, and 11315.

[7] Executive Order 13103, *Computer Software Piracy* (September 30, 1998).

[8] Executive Order 13589, *Promoting Efficient Spending* (November 9, 2011).

According to the Information Technology Infrastructure Library's *Guide to Software Asset Management*, software licenses are legal rights to use software in accordance with terms and conditions specified by the software copyright owner. [9] Rights to use software are separate from the legal rights to the software itself, which are normally kept by the software manufacturer or other third party. Licenses may be bought and are normally required whenever externally acquired software is used, which will typically be when the software is installed on a computer (or when executed on a computer even if installed elsewhere such as on a server). They may also be defined in enterprise terms, such as number of workstations or employees, in which case a license is required for each qualifying unit or individual regardless of actual usage.

Many software products are commercial-off-the-shelf, meaning the software is sold in substantial quantities in the commercial market place. Commercial software typically includes fees for initial and continued use of licenses. These fees may include, as part of the license contract, access to product support and/or other services, including upgrades.

Licensing models and definitions may significantly differ depending on the software product and vendor. For example, the guide[10] states that the basic types of licenses vary by duration and measure of usage:

Duration

- *Perpetual licenses*: These licenses are when use rights are permanent once purchased.

- *Subscription or rental licenses*: These licenses are used for a specific period of time, which can vary from days to years and may or may not include upgrade rights.

- *Temporary licenses*: These licenses are pending full payment or receipt of proof of purchase.

---

[9]Colin Rudd, *ITIL v.3 Guide to Software Asset Management* © *(2009), ISBN 9780113311064*. Reprinted with permission from ITIL. The guide is available at: http://www.axelos.com/Publications-Library/IT-Service-Management-ITIL/.

[10]Colin Rudd, *ITIL v.3 Guide to Software Asset Management* © *(2009), ISBN 9780113311064*. Reprinted with permission from ITIL. The guide is available at: http://www.axelos.com/Publications-Library/IT-Service-Management-ITIL/.

Measure of Use

- *Per copy, by workstation/seat/device, name used, anonymous user, or concurrent user.* Historically most licenses sold have been on a per-copy-used basis, with several different units of measure possible. Sometimes multiple users will be allowed per license

- *Concurrent usage*: This type of license allows a specified number of users to connect simultaneously to a software application. Products exist to help monitor and control concurrent usage; however, concurrent licenses are not as commonly available as per copy licenses.

- *Per server speed or per processor.* These licenses are linked to the speed or power of the server on which they run, or the number of processors within the server.

- *Enterprise or site*: These licenses are sold on an enterprise or site basis that requires a count of qualifying entities.

- *Other complexities*: Other, more complex licensing situations related to usage also exist with regard to licensing and the use of techniques such as multiplexing, clustering, virtualization, shared services, thin client, roaming services, and cloud and grid computing.

The objective of software license management is to manage, control, and protect an organization's software assets, including management of the risks arising from the use of those software assets.[11] Proper management of software licenses helps to minimize risks by ensuring that licenses are used in compliance with licensing agreements and cost-effectively deployed, and that software purchasing and maintenance expenses are properly controlled. To help ensure that the legal agreements that come with procured software licenses are adhered to and that organizations avoid purchasing unnecessary licenses, proper management of licenses is essential.

---

[11]Colin Rudd, *ITIL v.3 Guide to Software Asset Management* © (2009), ISBN *9780113311064*. Reprinted with permission from ITIL. The guide is available at: http://www.axelos.com/Publications-Library/IT-Service-Management-ITIL/.

GAO-14-413 Federal Software Licenses

OMB and Federal Agencies Need to Improve Policies on Managing Software Licenses

OMB and most federal agencies that we reviewed do not have adequate policies for managing software licenses. OMB has a broader IT management initiative, known as PortfolioStat, which is intended to assist agencies in gathering information on their IT investments, including software licenses. However, OMB does not have a directive guiding agencies in developing comprehensive software license management policies. Further, while 2 agencies have adequate policies for managing software licenses, the vast majority of agencies do not. Specifically, of the 24 major federal agencies, 18 have developed them, but they are not comprehensive; and 4 agencies have not developed any. The lack of robust licensing policies is due in part to the absence of direction from OMB. Without guidance from OMB or comprehensive policies, it will be difficult for the agencies to consistently and effectively manage software licenses.

Key OMB Policy Does Not Adequately Address Agencies' Software License Management

OMB has developed policy that addresses software licenses as part of its broader PortfolioStat IT initiative, as well as an executive order[12] containing additional direction to the agencies. Specifically, OMB launched the PortfolioStat initiative in March 2012, and it requires agencies to conduct an annual, agency-wide IT portfolio review to, among other things, reduce commodity IT[13] spending and demonstrate how their IT investments align with the agency's mission and business functions.[14] Toward this end, OMB established several key requirements for agencies, including designating a lead official with responsibility for implementing the process and consolidating at least two duplicative commodity IT areas; such areas could include software licenses.

PortfolioStat is also intended to assist agencies in meeting the targets and requirements under other OMB initiatives aimed at eliminating waste and duplication and promoting shared services across the federal

---

[12]Executive Order 13589, *Promoting Efficient Spending* (November 9, 2011), as previously discussed in this report.

[13]According to OMB, commodity IT includes services such as IT infrastructure (software licenses, data centers, networks, desktop computers and mobile devices); enterprise IT systems (e-mail, collaboration tools, identity and access management, security, and web infrastructure); and business systems (finance, human resources, and other administrative functions).

[14]OMB, *Implementing PortfolioStat*, Memorandum M-12-10 (Washington, D.C.: Mar. 30, 2012).

GAO-14-413 Federal Software Licenses

government, such as the Federal Strategic Sourcing Initiative.[15] For example, through the PortfolioStat process, OMB works with agencies to improve agency IT procurement processes, as outlined in the Federal Strategic Sourcing Initiative, in order to reduce prices on specific commodities that agency IT managers acquire, including software licenses.

However, it is up to the agencies to decide whether software licenses should be a priority for consolidation during the PortfolioStat review. Several agencies identified enterprise software licensing as a target area for cost savings or avoidance in the plans they provided to OMB in September 2012: the Department of Housing and Urban Development (HUD), the Department of State (State), the Department of Homeland Security (DHS), and the Department of Veterans Affairs (VA).

Further, while PortfolioStat can assist agencies in identifying cost savings and avoidance related to software licensing, this initiative, combined with the key executive order on more efficient software spending, is not enough to guide the agencies in developing comprehensive licensing management policies. As previously discussed, the executive order requires agencies to establish controls to ensure that they are not paying for unused or underutilized software. However, OMB lacks a directive that guides the agencies to ensure that they have appropriate policies.

An official from OMB's Office of E-Government and Information Technology stated that the PortfolioStat effort is intentionally focused on the organization as opposed to an individual area such as software license management. This official added that they have no plans to develop such guidance at this time.

Until the agencies have sufficient direction from OMB, opportunities to systematically identify software license related cost savings across the federal government will likely continue to be missed.

---

[15]In 2005, OMB directed federal agencies to develop and implement a strategic sourcing effort to help control spending. Strategic sourcing is a process that moves a company away from numerous individual procurements to a broader aggregate approach. A government-wide strategic sourcing program—known as the Federal Strategic Sourcing Initiative—was also established. The program management office for this initiative is located within the General Services Administration, and the program reports to OMB's Office of Federal Procurement Policy.

GAO-14-413 Federal Software Licenses

The Majority of Agencies Have Software License Management Policies, but They Are Not Comprehensive

Given the absence of an OMB directive providing guidance to agencies on licensing management policy, we identified seven elements[16] that a comprehensive software licensing policy should specify:

- identify clear roles, responsibilities, and central oversight authority within the department for managing enterprise software license agreements and commercial software licenses;

- establish a comprehensive inventory (80 percent of software license spending and/or enterprise licenses in the department) by identifying and collecting information about software license agreements using automated discovery and inventory tools;

- regularly track and maintain software licenses to assist the agency in implementing decisions throughout the software license management life cycle;

- analyze software usage and other data to make cost-effective decisions;

- provide training relevant to software license management;

- establish goals and objectives of the software license management program; and

- consider the software license management life-cycle phases (i.e., requisition, reception, deployment and maintenance, retirement, and disposal phases) to implement effective decision making and incorporate existing standards, processes, and metrics.

The following table provides a composite assessment of the 24 agencies' policies on managing software license against the seven elements.

---

[16]We identified these elements by interviewing six recognized software license management experts from the private and federal sectors and then comparing and synthesizing the information. See appendix I for more information on our methodology.

Table 1: Composite GAO Assessment of 24 Agencies' Policies on Managing Software Licenses

Agency	Assessment
Department of Agriculture	◐
Department of Commerce	∴
Department of Defense	◐
Department of Education	◐
Department of Energy	◐
Department of Health and Human Services	∴
Department of Homeland Security	●
Department of Housing and Urban Development	◐
Department of the Interior	∴
Department of Justice	◐
Department of Labor	●
Department of State	◐
Department of the Treasury	◐
Department of Transportation	◐
Department of Veterans Affairs	◐
Environmental Protection Agency	◐
General Services Administration	◐
National Aeronautics and Space Administration	◐
National Science Foundation	∴
Nuclear Regulatory Commission	◐
Office of Personnel Management	◐
Small Business Administration	◐
Social Security Administration	◐
U.S. Agency for International Development	◐

Source: GAO analysis of agency data.

Key:

● Fully—the agency provided evidence that it fully addressed the seven elements of a comprehensive software license policy.

◐ Partially—the agency provided evidence that it addressed some, but not all, of the seven elements of a comprehensive license policy.

∴ Not—the agency did not provide any evidence that it addressed any of the seven elements of a comprehensive license policy.

Two of the 24 agencies have developed comprehensive policies for managing software licenses, the Department of Labor (Labor) and DHS. For example, in April 2013, Labor's Office of the CIO software license management policies documented, among other things, how the agency manages installation requests and licensing of software that is applicable to its office and customers, as well as how licenses become part of its inventory. Similarly, in February 2012, DHS provided guidance that the Office of the CIO will monitor agency component usage of the enterprise license agreement software transfer process, refine the process as needed, and ensure cost avoidances are achieved. Related guidance also directs all DHS components, directorates, and offices not to use other contracting vehicles to procure software licenses once enterprise licenses are in place DHS-wide.

Further, 18 agencies have taken steps to include software license management policies in their IT management policies and procedures. However, inclusion of the seven elements we identified varied with each agency. Appendix II provides detailed information describing the extent to which the 18 agencies had comprehensive policies, and the following are illustrative examples.

- Defense established policies that include the establishment of a comprehensive inventory of software licenses and the analysis of these data to inform investment decisions to identify opportunities to reduce costs, but the department has not developed policies on centralizing management, tracking an inventory using automated tools, providing training to appropriate personnel on managing these licenses, or considering the software license management life-cycle phases.

- State has policies that identify agency responsibilities regarding the management of Microsoft and Oracle enterprise license agreements and the tracking of software licenses, but has not developed a policy for establishing a comprehensive inventory, analyzing software license data to inform investment decisions, providing training on management of software licenses, establishing goals and objectives of managing software licenses, and considering the software license management life-cycle phases.

- The Environmental Protection Agency (EPA) has policies at the business-unit level that address centralized management, establishing inventories, and tracking software licenses using tools; however, the agency has not developed a policy for analyzing software license data to inform decision making, providing training on managing software licenses, establishing goals and objectives for managing licenses, or considering the software license management life-cycle phases.

Finally, 4 agencies (the Department of Commerce (Commerce), the Department of Health and Human Services (HHS), the Department of the Interior (Interior), and the National Science Foundation (NSF)) had not developed department-wide policies for managing software licenses, according to officials. In one example, Commerce stated that it does not have policies at the department level, but instead the individual components are responsible for managing software licenses at the bureau level and may have issued relevant software license management policies. As an additional example, HHS has not established policies for managing software licenses, but stated that it plans to establish a vendor management office that will develop and manage guidance for centrally managing its software licenses.

The general consensus of the agency officials we spoke to on their policy weaknesses was that they were due, in part, to the lack of a priority for establishing or enhancing department- or agency-level software license management. As noted earlier, more specific direction from OMB could assist agencies in giving more adequate attention to this area. Until agencies develop comprehensive policies related to managing software licenses, they cannot ensure that they are consistently and cost-effectively managing software throughout the agency.

Federal Agencies' Practices on Managing Software Licenses Have Significant Weaknesses

Federal agencies are generally not following the leading practices we identified for managing their software licenses.[17] These practices include: centralizing management; establishing a comprehensive inventory of licenses; regularly tracking and maintaining comprehensive inventories using automated discovery and inventory tools and metrics; analyzing the software license data to inform investment decisions and identify opportunities to reduce costs; and providing appropriate personnel with sufficient training on software license management. Table 2 describes these leading practices in managing software licenses.

---

[17]We identified five leading practices for software license management by interviewing six recognized software license management experts from the private and federal sectors and then comparing and synthesizing the practices that were identified. See appendix I for more information on our methodology.

Table 2: Leading Practices for Managing Software Licenses

Leading practice	Description
Centralize management of software licenses	Employ a centralized software license management approach that is coordinated and integrated with key personnel (e.g., the acquisition and IT management personnel responsible for software purchases and decisions). Such an approach allows for centralized record keeping of software licensing details including the terms of the licenses. Further, agencies should centralize the governance and oversight of specific enterprise and commercial software licenses consistent with agency policy (e.g., software licenses reflective of the majority (80 percent) of agency software license spending and/or agency enterprise licenses) in order to make department-wide decisions.
Establish a comprehensive inventory of software licenses	Establish a comprehensive inventory of the software licenses consistent with agency policy (e.g., an inventory representative of majority (80 percent) of the agency's software license spending and/or enterprise licenses). This inventory should incorporate automated discovery and inventory tools that provide easy search and access to software license information (e.g., contract terms and agreement records). Such a repository allows managers to monitor performance (e.g., how many employees are using software compared to the amount of software purchased) and conduct analysis reporting needed for management decision making. A comprehensive inventory will better ensure compliance with software license agreements, and allow for agency-wide visibility that consolidates redundant applications and identification of other cost-saving opportunities.
Regularly track and maintain comprehensive inventories of software licenses using automated discovery and inventory tools and metrics	Regularly track and maintain comprehensive inventories of software licenses using automated discovery and inventory tools and metrics (e.g., metrics related to employee usage and number of licenses purchased) to ensure that the agency has the appropriate number of licenses for each item of software in use to reconcile with current use. Agencies should track inventories and compare software licenses purchased with licenses installed regularly (e.g., at least annually) and consistent with their policies.
Analyze the software license data to inform investment decisions and identify opportunities to reduce costs	Make decisions about software license investments that are informed by an analysis of department-wide software license data (e.g., costs, benefits, usage, and trending data). Such an analysis helps agencies make cost-effective decisions, including decisions about what users need.
Provide appropriate agency personnel with sufficient software license management training	Provide appropriate agency personnel (e.g., legal, acquisition, technical, and user) with sufficient training on managing software licenses, including training on contract terms and conditions, negotiations, laws and regulations, acquisition, security planning, and configuration management. Sufficient training allows organizations to develop the skills and knowledge of employees so they can perform their roles effectively and efficiently.

Source: GAO analysis of agency and expert data.

Of the 24 major federal agencies, 4 had fully demonstrated at least one of the leading practices, and none of the agencies had implemented all of the leading practices. Table 3 outlines the extent to which each of the 24 major federal agencies have implemented leading practices for managing software licenses. Following the table is a summary of the agencies' implementation of each key practice. Additional details on the 24 agencies are provided in appendix II.

Table 3: GAO Assessment of the 24 Agencies' Software License Management Practices

Agency	Centralized software license management approach	Comprehensive inventory established	Regular tracking and maintaining inventory using tools and metrics	Analysis of software license data	Sufficient training on software license management
Department of Agriculture	◐	◐	◐	◐	∴
Department of Commerce	∴	∴	∴	◐	∴
Department of Defense	◐	◐	◐	∴	◐
Department of Education	◐	◐	◐	◐	◐
Department of Energy	◐	◐	◐	∴	∴
Department of Health and Human Services	∴	∴	∴	∴	∴
Department of Homeland Security	◐	◐	◐	◐	◐
Department of Housing and Urban Development	●	●	◐	∴	∴
Department of the Interior	∴	◐	◐	◐	∴
Department of Justice	◐	◐	◐	∴	∴
Department of Labor	◐	◐	◐	∴	∴
Department of State	◐	◐	◐	◐	∴
Department of the Treasury	∴	◐	◐	∴	∴
Department of Transportation	◐	◐	◐	◐	∴
Department of Veterans Affairs	◐	◐	◐	◐	∴
Environmental Protection Agency	∴	◐	∴	∴	∴
General Services Administration	●	◐	◐	◐	∴
National Aeronautics and Space Administration	◐	◐	◐	◐	◐
National Science Foundation	●	●	◐	◐	∴
Nuclear Regulatory Commission	◐	◐	◐	◐	◐
Office of Personnel Management	◐	◐	◐	◐	∴
Small Business Administration	◐	◐	∴	∴	∴
Social Security Administration	◐	◐	◐	◐	∴
U.S. Agency for International Development	●	◐	◐	◐	∴

Source: GAO analysis of agency data.

Key:

● Fully met—the agency provided evidence that it fully addressed the leading practice.

◐ Partially met—the agency provided evidence that it addressed some, but not all, portions of the leading practice.

∴ Not met—the agency did not provide any evidence that it addressed the leading practice.

The majority of agencies have a partially centralized approach to managing software licenses. Four of the 24 agencies have a centralized approach to managing the majority (80 percent) of agency software license spending, and/or agency enterprise licenses; 15 agencies have a partially centralized approach; and 5 agencies have a decentralized approach to managing software licenses. For example, NSF manages licenses for enterprise-wide software in a centralized manner, which accounts for the majority of software used at the agency. Management of licenses for special-use software is decentralized, but it accounts for about 10 percent of the agency's overall software inventory.

With regard to the 15 with a partially centralized approach, these agencies may manage enterprise license agreements for selected software centrally, but other software, which accounts for the bulk of software used, may be managed by either agency components or individual program areas. For example, Labor manages all of the agency's Microsoft enterprise license agreements and other software managed within the Office of the CIO. However, Labor stated it does not track software licenses of other agency components. To better centralize the management of software licenses, Labor stated that it is in the process of combining all IT components and management of their software within the Office of the CIO and this effort is expected to be completed in fiscal year 2016.

The 5 agencies that have a decentralized approach for managing software licenses have delegated responsibilities to the components or individual program areas. For example, Commerce manages software licenses in a decentralized manner, where management of software licenses is delegated to the agency's components, and the management structure within these components may vary. Agency officials stated that in some components the Office of CIO is responsible for managing software licenses, whereas other Commerce components operate in an even more decentralized manner, with individual offices being responsible for managing software licenses. However, of these five agencies, officials from two agencies (HHS and Interior) noted they are planning to move toward centralizing their approach to managing software licenses.

The majority of agencies do not have comprehensive inventories of software licenses. Two of the 24 agencies have a comprehensive inventory of software licenses; 20 have some form of an inventory; and 2 do not have any inventory of their software licenses purchased. Specifically, according to HUD and NSF software license documentation, these agencies have a comprehensive inventory of software licenses that consists of the majority of the agency's spending on software licenses and/or enterprise licenses.

Twenty agencies have some form of an inventory, but they do not include the majority of the software license spending or number of licenses. For example, Energy has an inventory of software licenses within the Office of the CIO that it stated represents approximately 6 percent of the total number of users department-wide. Similarly, the Small Business Administration (SBA) has a centrally managed inventory, but the inventory is not comprehensive since it excludes information from several program offices. However, according to SBA officials, the agency has a tool to discover all software licenses on the SBA network that it expects to deploy later in fiscal year 2014.

The remaining 2 agencies do not have any inventory representing the majority of software license spending or total licenses.

The majority of agencies are partially tracking and managing software license deployment and usage. None of the 24 agencies are fully tracking and maintaining software license inventories. Specifically, 20 are partially tracking and managing licenses using automated discovery and inventory tools and metrics, and 4 do not track or manage software licenses with automated tools. Overall, agencies' tracking and managing of inventories varies. For example, the Department of Agriculture (USDA) uses two automated discovery and inventory tools to capture configuration information for all end points across the department to include desktops, laptops, and servers. However, officials from the Office of the CIO noted that these reports are not produced on a regular basis and the agency is not able to track software licenses outside of enterprise license agreements. As another example, according to DHS officials, the agency does not track comprehensive inventories using automated tools and metrics, but they stated that agency components track software outside of DHS's enterprise license agreements. However, DHS officials stated that DHS does not have visibility of the majority of the department's licenses. Additionally, Interior is using an automated discovery and inventory tool to track 21 different applications and operating systems. According to agency officials, Interior also uses spreadsheets to manually track licenses. However, the agency is not frequently tracking, managing, and reporting on the majority of software licenses.

Four agencies are not tracking and maintaining their inventories using automated discovery and inventory tools.

Agencies are not adequately analyzing data to identify opportunities for cost savings in software license purchases. None of the 24 agencies are fully analyzing software license data to inform investment decisions: 15 have analyzed some data to inform investment decisions or identify software license contract savings opportunities department-wide, and the remaining 9 have not assessed any software license data to identify opportunities for cost savings. More specifically, while the 15 agencies do not have controls in place for analyzing data on a regular basis, they are finding opportunities in an ad hoc manner to reduce software license spending and duplication. For example:

- Through OMB's PortfolioStat process, Commerce reported achieving a total of $1.05 million in cost savings in fiscal year 2012 through consolidation of selected software contracts, taking advantage of lower prices offered through enterprise licensing.

- DHS conducted department-wide contract business case assessments on re-competing Adobe enterprise license agreements. Based on the analyses, the agency reported cost avoidance over $125 million through the Adobe agreement from March 2010 through December 31, 2012. As another example, DHS negotiated more than 10 enterprise licensing agreements[18] with major software and hardware vendors, which led to cost avoidance of $181 million in fiscal year 2012. Furthermore, through the PortfolioStat process, in October 2012, the agency reported a total estimated savings or cost avoidance of approximately $376 million from fiscal year 2013 to fiscal year 2015 with its enterprise license agreement initiative.

- According to National Aeronautics and Space Administration (NASA) officials, in fiscal year 2013, the agency realized cost savings of approximately $33 million by consolidating major IT contracts, including Cisco and Microsoft licenses, to achieve efficiencies.

- VA reported through the PortfolioStat process that it renegotiated a fiscal year 2012 enterprise license agreement to reduce costs associated with software products used, saving the agency approximately $13 million in net cost avoidance in fiscal year 2012 and $37 million in net cost avoidance for fiscal year 2013.

---

[18]Enterprise-wide agreements are contracts that are at the department or agency level.

- State reported through the PortfolioStat process a total estimated savings or cost avoidance of $6 million for fiscal years 2014 and 2015 with regard to enterprise licensing software.

The remaining agencies did not demonstrate that they had analyzed software license data to inform investment decisions. For example, Department of Justice officials stated that this is primarily performed as subordinate activities within programs or as annual activities for software renewal through contract negotiations. However, documentation of this analysis was not provided.

The majority of agencies lack training on management of software licenses. None of the 24 agencies provided sufficient training to appropriate personnel on managing software licenses. Specifically, 5 provided some, but not all, key training on managing software licenses, including contract terms and conditions, and 19 did not provide any software licenses management training. Specifically, in April 2013, NASA provided a webinar presentation on its Enterprise License Management Team that included information on the program's mission, objectives, dependencies and interfaces, and business cases, among other things. However, this training did not include aspects of sufficient software license management training such as negotiations, laws and regulations, and contract terms and conditions department-wide. Similarly, while NRC has provided software license management training to employees related to configuration management through its broader training on Information Technology Infrastructure Library, it has not done so for contract terms and conditions as well as negotiations of software license agreements. While these agencies have taken positive steps, the vast majority of the federal agencies lack sufficient training.

The inadequate implementation of leading practices in software license management can be linked to the weaknesses in agencies' policies and decentralized approaches to license management. As a result, agencies' oversight of software license spending has been limited or lacking. Therefore, without improved policies and oversight, agencies will likely miss opportunities for significant savings across the federal government.

Agencies' Most Widely Used Software Applications Are Not Known Due to Data Limitations

Given the weaknesses identified in this report regarding agencies' lack of comprehensive, well-maintained inventories of software licenses, we cannot accurately describe the most widely used software applications across the government, including the extent to which they were over and under purchased. Further, the data provided by agencies regarding their most widely used applications are varying, incomplete, or not available—and thus, cannot be compared across the government.

Varying data: The agencies that had data on widely used software applications provided it in various ways, including by license count, usage, and cost. For example:

- **State, General Services Administration (GSA), and Labor provided data by both license count and cost.** According to a State official, in fiscal year 2013, the cost for the department's most widely used software applications was about $17 million. Officials also stated that Microsoft Office Professional 2010 is the costliest application for the department (about $7 million) and Entrust Entelligence Security Provider is the most widely used application by licenses (approximately 124,000 licenses, costing about $436,000). GSA provided a list of 13,809 different applications with total software licenses counts for each specific application. According to the agency, in fiscal year 2013, Oracle was the costliest application (about $5.4 million), and Extend360 Enforcement Agent was the agency's most widely used application, with about 17,430 licenses. According to GSA officials, in fiscal year 2013, the cost for the most widely used software applications by license count was about $13 million. Furthermore, Labor reported that its most widely used software applications costs about $1.1 million in fiscal year 2012. In addition, Labor reported that Windows 7 bundled with Microsoft Office Professional 2010 was the department's most costly software (approximately $427,000 with 3,050 users). On the other hand, SCCM Advanced Client was the department's most common software, with 3,107 users and costing about $41,000.

- **NASA and OPM provided data by cost.** Specifically, NASA and OPM reported on their costliest applications and stated that the most widely used applications by license count and cost are the same. In particular, OPM reported that its most widely used applications cost about $9.7 million in fiscal year 2013. Among these, OPM reported its Microsoft and Oracle enterprise licenses agreement are the most costly applications with about $2.1 million for each application, but no data on license count was provided. NASA reported that in fiscal year 2012 the agency spent about $13 million on its most widely used applications. Among these, NASA reported that Oracle is the most widely used application by both license count and cost. In fiscal year 2012, the agency spent approximately $4.6 million on this software for 122,279 licenses.

- **U.S. Agency for International Development (USAID) and Treasury provided data by license count.** USAID reported Microsoft Configuration Manager Client as its most widely used application, with 12,341 licenses, but no cost data were provided. Similarly, Treasury reported Microsoft as its most widely used application, with about 1.3 million licenses, but no further data were provided on actual applications, and department officials stated it does not maintain a list of the most costly applications; rather it uses the procurement process as an opportunity to reassess software needs.

- **USDA provided data on license usage**. Specifically, these data included the total number of computers and the total number of times the software was used. For example Microsoft Corporation was listed, with 124,310 computers and 83,542,797 total instances in which the software was used; however, further data were not provided on the use of the actual applications (i.e., the number of instances in which the software was used or the total of duration of time it was used).

Incomplete data: The data provided by the agencies on the most widely used applications were not always complete. For example, EPA's reported data included count and cost for a subset of software, and therefore it was unclear which applications were most widely used. In addition, while ten agencies (Commerce, the Department of Transportation (DOT), Education, the Department of Energy (Energy), Interior, Justice, NRC, SBA, and the Social Security Administration (SSA)) provided a list of most widely used applications, no specific usage data on the number of instances in which the software was used, the total of duration of time it was used, or no cost was provided.

Unavailable data: Four agencies (Defense, HHS, DHS and VA) did not have available data on the most widely used applications. The agencies cited various reasons for not having these data, or for having incomplete data. These reasons included non-centralized management of software licenses and not having validated, reliable information. For example, HHS indicated that these data are not available because the operating divisions manage their own software applications. Similarly, according to DHS officials, to provide the data on its most widely used and costliest applications would require a larger departmental effort, including a data call to each of the components. In addition, VA indicated that it is in the process of validating this information and could not provide an accurate answer.

As for the extent to which most widely used software licenses were over and under purchased, none of the 24 agencies had cost data available for over- or under-purchasing of their most widely used software applications. Three agencies provided partial information on over- or under-purchasing for the most widely used applications: Defense, SBA, and USDA. Specifically, Defense officials stated that information on over- or under-purchasing exists within the Department of the Army for Microsoft products; however, no data were provided. SBA believes this figure is under $75,000 annually but did not have documentation to support this assertion. Also, according to USDA officials, for fiscal year 2014, the agency reduced its Microsoft Desktop licensing by over 4,000 units for the new contract renewal and 11,000 for Adobe Acrobat Standard software. However, the remaining 21 agencies do not have information on over- or under-purchasing for the most widely used applications. For example, Commerce officials stated they are not aware of any over- or under-purchased software and attributed this to a decentralized approach to managing licenses. In addition, USAID officials stated that reporting on over- and under-purchased licenses is problematic because of the manual efforts that are required to gather and compare data against known purchases. GSA officials stated that GSA does not have this information available; however, they indicated that GSA plans to form an office tasked with this responsibility.

Until agencies address the weaknesses identified in how they manage their software licenses, including establishing a comprehensive inventory that is regularly tracked and maintained, the most widely used applications across the federal government cannot be accurately determined. Additionally, because agencies were unable to identify the extent to which these applications were over or under purchased, they risk procuring software in a costly and ineffective manner.

Conclusions

The federal government procures thousands of software licenses agreements annually, and therefore effectively managing them is critical to ensure that agencies maximize the value of these investments. OMB has issued a policy associated with a broader IT management initiative but does not have a directive that assists agencies in developing licensing policies. This is especially important since the majority of agencies lack comprehensive policies and have significant weaknesses in managing their software licenses. While most agencies have established policies that address leading practices for effectively managing software licenses, they are not comprehensive. This has contributed to the majority of agencies (1) not having a fully centralized approach for managing licenses, (2) not fully establishing a comprehensive inventory for regularly tracking and maintaining software licenses, (3) not regularly tracking and maintaining an inventory using tools and metrics, or (4) not providing sufficient training on software management. The result is an inability to analyze software license data to more cost-effectively buy and maintain software licenses, and ascertain the software applications most widely used across the federal government. Consequently, while agencies were able to identify millions in savings for software, there is the potential for even greater savings and additional opportunities to reduce software license spending and duplication than what agencies have reported. Until OMB and the agencies focus on improving policies and processes, they will not have the data to manage software licenses and will likely miss opportunities to reduce costs.

Recommendations for Executive Action

We recommend that the Director of OMB issue a directive to the agencies on developing comprehensive software licensing policies comprised of the seven elements identified in this report.

We are also making numerous recommendations to the 24 departments and agencies in our review to improve their policies and practices for managing software licenses. Appendix III contains these recommendations.

Agency Comments and Our Evaluation

We provided a draft of this report to OMB and the 24 Chief Financial Officers Act agencies in our review for comment and received responses from all 25. OMB disagreed with our recommendation to issue a directive and of the 24 agencies that we made specific recommendations to, 11 agreed, 5 partially agreed, 2 neither agreed nor disagreed, and 6 had no comments. The agencies' comments and our responses are summarized below.

- In written comments, OMB noted that there are several management tools in place with respect to software license management, including the three we identified in our report; however, the agency disagreed with our statements that OMB and federal agencies need to improve policies on managing software licenses, and that until agencies have sufficient direction from OMB, opportunities to systematically identify software license related cost savings across the federal government will likely continue to be missed. In particular, OMB cited two additional management initiatives that it asserted have significant bearing in the area of software licensing that were not included in our report. These two initiatives are known as "Maximizing Use of SmartBuy and Avoiding Duplication" and "Cross Agency Priority Goal: Cybersecurity."

OMB stated that the SmartBuy initiative, along with the initiatives detailed in our report, deliver a policy foundation that allows an agency to leverage GSA and collaborate with agencies and monitor performance. In addition, OMB stated that the Cybersecurity initiative can be used to understand the risk and vulnerabilities of the software an agency is using. The agency also noted that through the collective OMB initiatives, agencies now have the tools to identify when there is underutilization of software and are better able to recapture those underutilized licenses and deploy them to people who need them.

While we agree that OMB's initiatives collectively represent important management tools for agencies, they are not enough to guide agencies in developing comprehensive license management policies. More specifically, the two initiatives along with the other three we previously cited do not provide guidance to agencies on developing software license management policies comprised of the seven elements identified in our report. Our report shows that only 2 of the 24 major agencies have comprehensive policies in place; and only 2 have comprehensive license inventories. Until this gap in guidance is addressed, agencies will likely continue to lack the visibility into what needs to be managed, and be unable to take full advantage of OMB's SmartBuy and other tools to drive license efficiency and utilization. Therefore, we continue to believe that OMB should develop a directive that guides the agencies to ensure that they have appropriate policies. OMB's comments are reprinted in appendix XX.

- In e-mail comments, an official from Agriculture's Audit Liaison Group stated that the department generally concurs with our findings and recommendations and plans to move forward with our recommendations.

- In written comments, Commerce stated the department concurred with our findings as they apply to the status of software license management within the department, but partially concurred with four of our six recommendations. Specifically, the department plans to develop an agency-wide comprehensive policy for the management of software licenses, and ensure that software license management training is provided to appropriate agency personnel. Since the department did not provide any information on the reasons why it partially concurred with the remaining recommendations, we are maintaining our recommendations. Commerce's comments are reprinted in appendix IV.

- In written comments, Defense concurred with two of the six recommendations and partially concurred with the remaining ones. Specifically, the department partially concurred with our recommendations to develop a comprehensive policy; employ a centralized license management approach; establish a comprehensive license inventory; and regularly track and maintain the inventory using automated tools and metrics.

   With regard to a need for a comprehensive policy and centralized approach, the department stated that it concurs that a license management policy is necessary to address the weaknesses we identified; and that the majority of license spending and/or enterprise-wide licenses should be managed using an approach that is coordinated and integrated with key personnel. However, Defense stated it does not concur that a centralized management approach is appropriate for the size and complexity of the department.

   We continue to believe our recommendations are valid because consistent with leading practices, in order to take advantage of economies of scale, a single entity should have access to department-wide software license data. Furthermore, the National Defense Authorization Act for Fiscal Year 2013 requires the Defense CIO, in consultation with Defense component CIOs, to issue a plan to conduct a department-wide inventory of a subset of software licenses that will maximize its return on investment; and to describe in the plan how the department can achieve the greatest economies of scale and savings in the procurement, use, and optimization of these licenses. In addition, the National Defense Authorization Act for Fiscal Year 2014 further clarifies what the plan should entail. Adequately conducting an inventory will necessitate that Defense centrally manage its software license data. Having licensing management policy in place to address the identified weaknesses, as well as employing a centralized approach, would position the department to more effectively carry out these mandated requirements, among other things.

With regard to the need for a license inventory and tools to track the inventory, Defense stated that it concurs that inventory data should be collected for agency software licenses purchased and/or enterprise-wide licenses; and that effective license management requires regular tracking and maintaining of inventory data using automated tools and metrics. However, the department stated it does not concur that maintaining an inventory comprising the majority of software regardless of dollar value is required. Further, Defense stated it may be resource exhaustive to incorporate automated tools to establish inventories for the majority of licenses; and may not be practicable to retroactively collect standard data about historical license transactions due to the decentralized nature of purchasing and license management today within the department.

We agree that inventory data does not need to include all software regardless of dollar value. As detailed in our report, leading practices note a comprehensive inventory should represent the majority (80 percent) of the agency's software license spending and/or enterprise licenses to allow the department visibility that reduces redundant applications and identification of other cost saving opportunities. Moreover, in response to the requirements in the National Defense Authorization Act for Fiscal Year 2013, Defense's own licensing inventory plan is based on the software products with the highest relative spend across the department to target the products that present the greatest potential economies of scale and cost savings. In other words, the department is already planning to take steps to establish an inventory consistent with our recommendation.

Regarding the use of automated tools to collect and maintain the licensing inventory, we agree that the department should take the most cost-effective and forward-looking approach. Accordingly, a focus on implementing tools and metrics on current and future software license purchases (rather than historical transactions) is reasonable. Such an approach is consistent with our recommendations; therefore, we are maintaining them. The department's comments are reprinted in appendix V.

- In written comments, Education concurred with our recommendations and stated it plans to implement a revised software acquisition policy in 2014, which will allow for better management, tracking, and reporting of software licenses. The department's comments are reprinted in appendix VI.

- In written comments, Energy neither agreed nor disagreed with our recommendations, but stated that it has taken a number of steps to aggregate licensing, and at this time has no plans to centralize software licensing. In particular, the department stated it agrees that there may be opportunities to aggregate licensing to achieve volume discounts and integrate disparate but related data sources. Energy further stated its IT Modernization Strategy, targeted for completion in fiscal year 2016, seeks to reduce the number of procurement vehicles and to leverage the department's collective buying power, among other things. Energy also described activities under way that it believes address our specific recommendations, as well as clarified specific facts (on developing a comprehensive policy and having visibility into 45 percent of the department's licenses), which we incorporated in the report as appropriate.

  While we agree that these activities are important steps, we continue to believe that further work is needed to improve software license management at the department. Because of Energy's decentralized approach, it does not have visibility into the majority of the department's software licenses. Additionally, while the department stated analysis is done on agency-wide software usage and training is managed on an office-by-office basis, Energy could not provide evidence to substantiate these claims. Until the department takes a more centralized approach, as well as addresses the other identified weaknesses, such as regular analysis of licensing inventory data to inform decisions and relevant management training, the department will likely not be adequately positioned to take advantage of the procurement vehicles and collective buying power currently being planned as part of its modernization strategy. The department's comments are reprinted in appendix VII.

- In written comments, HHS neither agreed nor disagreed with our recommendations and noted initiatives it plans to take to promote cost savings and visibility regarding IT spending. The department's comments are reprinted in appendix VIII.

- In written comments, DHS concurred with our recommendations and identified steps the department plans to take to address the weaknesses. The department's comments are reprinted in appendix IX.

GAO-14-413 Federal Software Licenses

- In written comments, HUD had no comments on our report and stated it would provide more definitive information with timelines once the final report has been issued. The department's comments are reprinted in appendix X.

- In written comments, Interior agreed with most of our findings and concurred with five recommendations and partially concurred with one recommendation. The department partially disagreed with our recommendation to provide sufficient software license management training to appropriate personnel, stating that it will continue to provide training on contract terms and conditions, among other things and it does not agree that unique training is needed for software license management. We agree that unique training in software license management is not needed if included as part of other training as we identified in our report. However, the department did not provide any documentation to support that training has been provided to appropriate personnel. We therefore maintain our recommendation. The department's comments are reprinted in appendix XI.

- In e-mail comments, an official from Justice's Audit Liaison Group stated that the department concurs with the recommendations and will address how it plans to implement them once the final report has been issued.

- In e-mail comments, an official from Labor's Office of the Assistant Secretary for Policy stated the department had no comments.

- In written comments, State noted that it concurred with our recommendations and plans to identify actions to address these recommendations. The department's comments are reprinted in appendix XII.

- In e-mail comments, the Deputy Director of Audit Relations from Transportation stated it had no comments.

- In written comments, the Department of the Treasury had no comments on the report. The department's comments are reprinted in appendix XIII.

- In written comments, VA generally agreed with our conclusions and concurred with our six recommendations. The department also identified initiatives underway to address the weaknesses identified in the report. The department's comments are reprinted in appendix XIV.

- In written comments, EPA partially agreed with our assessment and acknowledges that there is work to be done to better manage software licenses for the agency. Since the agency did not specifically state why it partially concurred, we are maintaining our recommendations. The agency's comments are reprinted in appendix XV.

- In written comments, GSA agreed with our findings and recommendations and stated it would take actions as appropriate. The agency's comments are reprinted in appendix XVI.

- In written comments, NASA concurred with three recommendations and partially concurred with three others. Specifically, the agency partially concurred with our recommendations to employ a centralized management approach, establish a comprehensive license inventory, and regularly track and maintain this inventory using automated tools and metrics. The agency stated that to fully implement a centralized software license management approach will require several phases, working with NASA stakeholders to ensure both mission and institutional software is integrated. In particular, NASA stated it would be difficult to employ one centralized software license management tool because, while it has a mechanism in place for a few of its large enterprise license purchases, several of its large IT contracts have purchasing of licenses embedded in the contract conditions. Accordingly, the agency cannot easily obtain inventory data for licenses not in its control (i.e., contractor-managed licenses). Additionally, NASA noted that to fully establish and regularly track and maintain a comprehensive inventory will require changes to some of the large IT contracts at the agency to be able to automatically pull the licensing information into a centralized system, with increased costs.

  While we agree that a phased approach to implementing a centralized software license approach may be the most practicable, we are not advocating the department collect information on licenses it does not control. Instead our recommendations to establish and regularly track and maintain a comprehensive inventory of licenses are for the licenses that NASA purchases directly, as we noted in our report. Thus, we maintain our recommendations. The agency's comments are reprinted in appendix XVII.

- In written comments, NSF stated that it had no comments on our report. The agency's comments are reprinted in appendix XVIII.

- In written comments, NRC stated it generally agreed with our report and had no further comments. The agency's comments are reprinted in appendix XIX.

- In written comments, OPM concurred with our recommendations and noted actions the agency plans to take. The agency's comments are reprinted in appendix XXI.

- In e-mail comments, an official from SBA's Office of Congressional and Legislative Affairs stated it had no comments.

- In written comments, SSA agreed with our recommendations and identified actions the agency plans to take. The agency's comments are reprinted in appendix XXII.

- In written comments, USAID agreed with our recommendations and identified actions it plans to take. The agency's comments are reprinted in appendix XXIII.

We are sending copies of this report to the appropriate congressional committees; the Secretaries of the Departments of Agriculture, Commerce, Defense, Education, Energy, Health and Human Services, Homeland Security, Housing and Urban Development, the Interior, Labor, State, Transportation, the Treasury, and Veterans Affairs; the Attorney General; the Administrator of the Environmental Protection Agency; the Administrator of the General Services Administration; the Administrator of the National Aeronautics and Space Administration; the Director of the National Science Foundation; the Chairman of the Nuclear Regulatory Commission; the Director of the Office of Management and Budget; the Director of the Office of Personnel Management; the Administrator of the Small Business Administration; the Commissioner of the Social Security Administration; the Administrator of the U.S. Agency for International Development; and other interested parties. This report also is available at no charge on the GAO website at http://www.gao.gov.

Should you or your staff have any questions on information discussed in this report, please contact me at (202) 512-4456 or ChaC@gao.gov. Contact points for our Offices of Congressional Relations and Public

Affairs may be found on the last page of this report. GAO staff who made major contributions to this report are listed in appendix XXIV.

Sincerely yours,

Carol R. Cha
Director
Information Technology Acquisition Management Issues

Appendix I: Objectives, Scope, and Methodology

Our objectives for this engagement were to (1) assess the extent to which the Office of Management and Budget (OMB) and federal agencies have appropriate policies on software license management, (2) determine the extent to which federal agencies are adequately managing software licenses, and (3) describe the software applications most widely used by the federal agencies and the extent to which they were over or under purchased. The scope of our review included the 24 major agencies covered by the Chief Financial Officers Act of 1990.[1]

To address our first objective, we identified seven elements that comprehensive software license policies should contain. To do so, we first identified experts in the field of software license management by reviewing software license management websites and professional literature. We then selected six experts based on type, depth, and relevance of software license management experience, as well as relevance of published work, awards and recognition in the professional community, recommendations, and availability with a range of private and public sector experience. We selected the following six individuals:

- Patricia Adams—Research Director, Gartner, Inc.
- Victoria Barber—Research Director, Gartner, Inc.
- Tim Clark—Partner, The FactPoint Group
- Steve Cooper—Chief Information Officer (CIO) Executive Advisor, Mason-Harriman Group and former Federal Aviation Administration CIO
- Mark Day—Deputy Assistant Commissioner, Office of Integrated Technology Services, General Services Administration
- Amy Konary—Research Vice President, International Data Corporation

Following our expert selection process, we interviewed each of the recognized experts to solicit information about what software license policies should contain.

---

[1]The 24 major federal agencies covered by the Chief Financial Officers Act of 1990 are the Departments of Agriculture, Commerce, Defense, Education, Energy, Health and Human Services, Homeland Security, Housing and Urban Development, the Interior, Justice, Labor, State, Transportation, the Treasury, and Veterans Affairs; Environmental Protection Agency; General Services Administration; National Aeronautics and Space Administration; National Science Foundation; Nuclear Regulatory Commission; Office of Personnel Management; Small Business Administration; Social Security Administration; and U.S. Agency for International Development.

We then compared the information collected from the experts against
OMB guidance,[2] relevant executive orders,[3] other federal guidance,[4] and
professional literature. We synthesized the resulting information into a list
of seven elements:

- identify clear roles, responsibilities, and central oversight authority
  within the department for managing enterprise software license
  agreements and commercial software licenses;

- establish a comprehensive inventory (80 percent of software license
  spending and/or enterprise licenses in the department) by identifying
  and collecting information about software license agreements using
  automated discovery and inventory tools;

- regularly track and maintain software licenses to assist the agency in
  implementing decisions throughout the software license management
  life cycle;

- analyze software usage and other data to make cost-effective
  decisions;

- provide training relevant to software license management;

- establish goals and objectives of the software license management
  program; and

- consider the software license management life-cycle phases (i.e.,
  requisition, reception, deployment and maintenance, retirement, and
  disposal phases) to implement effective decision making and
  incorporate existing standards, processes, and metrics.

---

[2]OMB, *Memorandum for Heads of Executive Departments and Agencies: Chief
Information Officer Authorities*, M-11-29 (Washington, D.C.: Aug. 08, 2011); and OMB,
*Memorandum for Chief Acquisition Officers Senior Procurement Executives: Achieving
Better Value from Our Acquisitions* (Washington, D.C.: Dec. 22, 2009).

[3]Executive Order No. 13589, *Promoting Efficient Spending* (Nov. 9, 2011); and Executive
Order 13103, *Computer Software Piracy* (Sept. 30, 1998).

[4]National Institute of Standards and Technology (NIST), *Recommended Security Controls
for Federal Information Systems and Organizations*, SP 800-53 Revision 3 (Gaithersburg,
Md.: August 2009); and NIST, *Information Technology Security Training Requirements: A
Role- and Performance-Based Model*, SP800-16 (Gaithersburg, Md.: April 1998).

We then solicited feedback from our experts on the elements developed, and integrated this feedback to finalize our elements. Three of the experts contributed to the validation of our list of elements.

For each of the 24 agencies, we then obtained and analyzed policy documents, such as agency and departmental guidance, policies, procedures, regulations, and standard operating procedures, and compared them to the seven elements. We also obtained information through interviews with officials responsible for software license management activities.

Further, to assess the extent to which the OMB has appropriate guidance on software license management, we collected and analyzed OMB guidance on the PortfolioStat and Strategic Sourcing initiatives to determine its efforts to oversee federal agencies' management of software licenses. We then compared these efforts to relevant legislation and executive orders. In addition, we reviewed the results of our prior work on PortfolioStat.[5] We then interviewed OMB officials to identify their views on whether the relevant guidance for software license management to federal agencies is appropriately established.

For our second objective, on managing licenses, we identified five leading practices in the field of software license management. We used the same process involving the six experts as described for the first objective. We synthesized the resulting information into a set of leading practices that can help agencies manage their software licenses, including (1) centralizing the management of software licenses; (2) establishing a comprehensive inventory that represents at least 80 percent of the agency's total software license spending and/or total software licenses agency-wide; (3) regularly tracking and maintaining an inventory using automated discovery and inventory tools and metrics; (4) analyzing the data to inform investment decisions and identifying opportunities to reduce costs; and (5) providing appropriate agency personnel with sufficient software license management training. We then solicited feedback from our experts on the leading practices developed, and integrated this feedback to finalize our leading practices. Three of these experts contributed to the validation of our list of effective practices.

---

[5]GAO, *Information Technology: Additional OMB and Agency Actions Are Needed to Achieve Portfolio Savings*, GAO-14-65 (Washington, D.C.: Nov. 6, 2013).

To determine the extent to which federal agencies are adequately
managing their software licenses, we obtained and analyzed relevant
software license information such as budget documentation for fiscal
years 2012 and 2013, software contracts, management of software
license policies and procedures, software license inventories for fiscal
years 2012 and 2013, documentation on internally reported cost saving,
training curriculums, software management application documentation
and reports. We also obtained information through interviews with officials
responsible for software license management activities. For each agency,
we then compared agencies' documentation against the five leading
practices to determine the extent to which they are adequately managing
licenses.

To assess the reliability of the data agencies provided in their software
license inventories, we confirmed with agencies whether these
inventories were comprehensive (i.e., representing at least 80 percent of
the agency's total software license spending and/or total software
licenses agency-wide). In cases where the agency attested to its being
comprehensive, we asked agency officials how they ensure the data
within their inventories are comprehensive, reliable, valid, and accurate,
and requested supporting documentation, such as those related to
internal control processes. For those inventories that agencies reported
as not comprehensive, we determined additional data reliability steps
were not required because agencies have knowledge to determine
whether they do not have a comprehensive inventory and would not have
concerns with inventories being rated as not comprehensive if the rating
was based on their own assessment. We concluded that the data were
sufficiently reliable for our purposes for the first two objectives.

Finally, for our third objective, we collected and analyzed information on
the most widely used software applications, such as agencies' software
inventories and/or lists of applications according to volume and spending.
In addition, we obtained information on whether software licenses were
over or under purchased for the most widely used applications, as
documented by the agencies. For each of the 24 agencies, we analyzed
the information to describe the extent to which the most widely used
applications were over or under purchased. We also interviewed agency
officials. We identified issues with the reliability of the information on the
most widely used applications because the data varied or were
incomplete. We did not test the adequacy of agencies' cost data. Our
evaluation of these cost data was based on what we were told by
agencies and the information the agencies could provide.

We conducted this performance audit from March 2013 to May 2014 in
accordance with generally accepted government auditing standards.
Those standards require that we plan and perform the audit to obtain
sufficient, appropriate evidence to provide a reasonable basis for our
findings and conclusions based on our audit objectives. We believe that
the evidence obtained provides a reasonable basis for our findings and
conclusions based on our audit objectives.

Appendix II: Detailed Assessments of Agencies' Software License Management Practices

We conducted detailed assessments of the 24 Chief Financial Officers Act agencies' software license management practices against leading practices. The following section summarizes the results of our assessment of each agency's software license management against leading practices.

Department of Agriculture

Table 4 provides a detailed summary of the results of our assessment of the Department of Agriculture's (USDA) practices for managing software licenses against leading practices.

Table 4: Assessment of Department of Agriculture's Practices for Managing Software Licenses

Leading practice	GAO assessment	Summary of evidence
Develop comprehensive policy for management of software licenses	◖	USDA has a draft policy supplemented by an approved policy that only applies to workstations managed by its Information Technology Services within the Office of the Chief Information Officer. Specifically, the draft policy and approved policy partially addresses centralized management, a comprehensive inventory, periodic reconciliation on license usage based on license tracking, analysis to inform investment decision making, goals and objectives, and management of licenses throughout the entire life cycle; however, it does not address education and training.
Centralized software license management approach	◖	According to USDA officials, the department manages software licenses for all enterprise agreements sponsored by its Office of the Chief Information Officer in a centralized manner, with some exceptions in which software licenses are purchased for very specific purposes. Approximately 45,000 of USDA's 130,000 workstations are managed centrally through the Office of the Chief Information Officer, and the primary focus is on high-dollar software license purchases, according to USDA officials.
Established comprehensive inventory	◖	USDA maintains an inventory of its software licenses for Adobe Acrobat, SAS, and AutoCAD software licenses; however, it is unclear if these inventories are comprehensive and represent the majority of licenses within the department.
Regularly tracking and maintaining inventory using tools and metrics	◖	USDA uses automated tools to track and manage software licenses, but is unable to track all procurement. Specifically, USDA uses automated tools to capture configuration information for all end points across the department to include desktops, laptops and servers. It also identifies software installed on the end points by publisher, title, and version, along with metrics on software utilization. According to officials, automated reports are used to validate the licenses in use against the enterprise license agreements sponsored by the Office of the Chief Information Officer. However, officials noted that these reports are not produced on a regular basis and the department is not able to track procurement outside of enterprise license agreements.
Analysis of software license data	◖	USDA conducted analysis of its software inventories for AutoDesk and Adobe products to inform investment decisions; however, it is unclear if this analysis was completed for other software vendors. For example, USDA officials indicated a reduction of approximately 2,500 AutoDesk licenses and 11,000 Adobe licenses as a result of this analysis. However, the results of this analysis for other vendors, such as Microsoft or Oracle, were not available, and it is unclear if these analyses for the other vendors have been completed.

Leading practice	GAO assessment	Summary of evidence
Sufficient training on software license management	∷	According to officials, training in software license management, if any, is provided at the agency level and may be covered as part of training on information technology (IT) management best practices. USDA's Office of the Chief Information Officer does not provide formal training in software license management.

Source: GAO analysis of USDA data.

Key:

● Fully met—the agency provided evidence that it fully addressed the leading practice.

◐ Partially met—the agency provided evidence that it addressed some, but not all, portions of the leading practice.

∷ Not met—the agency did not provide any evidence that it addressed the leading practice.

Department of Commerce

Table 5 provides a detailed summary of the results of our assessment of the Department of Commerce's (Commerce) practices for managing software licenses against leading practices.

Table 5: Assessment of Department of Commerce's Practices for Managing Software Licenses

Leading practice	GAO assessment	Summary of evidence
Develop comprehensive policy for management of software licenses.	∷	According to Commerce officials, the department has not developed comprehensive policies for management of software licenses at the department level. Commerce officials stated individual components are responsible for managing software licenses at the bureau level, but this responsibility has not been formally documented. In addition, according to Commerce officials, individual components may have issued relevant software license management policies.
Centralized software license management approach	∷	According to Commerce officials, the department manages software licenses in a decentralized manner, where management of software licenses is delegated to the department's components. Commerce officials also stated that components' software license management structure may vary. For example, the officials stated that in some components the Office of the Chief Information Officer is responsible for managing software licenses, whereas other Commerce components operate in a decentralized manner, with individual offices being responsible for managing software licenses.
Established comprehensive inventory	∷	A Commerce official stated the department has not established a comprehensive inventory of software; however, some components have inventories that have varying degrees of completeness.
Regularly tracking and maintaining inventory using tools and metrics	∷	Commerce does not track and maintain comprehensive inventories using automated tools and metrics. A Commerce official explained that components have responsibility for managing software and some components may track and maintain inventories.

Leading practice	GAO assessment	Summary of evidence
Analysis of software license data	◐	Commerce officials stated that while the department has not conducted a systematic analysis of software license data department-wide, it has analyzed several software product areas to inform investment decisions to reduce costs. For example Commerce officials stated that it has conducted analyses focused on Adobe, Microsoft, and Endpoint protection software suites to make relevant investment decisions and to identify opportunities to reduce costs. For example, by analyzing Adobe software and pricing in March 2012, Commerce was able to conclude that by establishing a department-wide Adobe enterprise license agreement and having agreement from all components, the department could reduce administrative burden and increase spending visibility through vendor reports. However, according to Commerce officials, the department has not analyzed all software licenses department-wide.
Sufficient training on software license management	∴	According to Commerce officials, the department has not provided training in the area of software license management.

Source: GAO analysis of Commerce data.

Key:

● Fully met—the agency provided evidence that it fully addressed the leading practice.

◐ Partially met—the agency provided evidence that it addressed some, but not all, portions of the leading practice.

∴ Not met—the agency did not provide any evidence that it addressed the leading practice.

Department of Defense

Table 6 provides a detailed summary of the results of our assessment of the Department of Defense's (Defense) practices for managing software licenses against leading practices.[1]

Table 6: Assessment of Department of Defense's Practices for Managing Software Licenses

Leading practice	GAO assessment	Summary of evidence
Develop comprehensive policy for management of software licenses	◐	Defense has policies that include the establishment of an inventory of software licenses and implementation and the analysis of this data to inform investment decisions and identify opportunities to reduce costs. However, Defense has not provided policy for the remaining leading practices, including centralized management, tracking an inventory using automated tools, education and training, and management of software license through the entire life cycle.

---

[1]We have ongoing work to review the department's assessment and performance plan for managing software licenses, as required by the National Defense Authorization Act for Fiscal Year 2013.

Leading practice	GAO assessment	Summary of evidence
Centralized software license management approach	◑	While Defense manages licenses at the component level, the components must consider the corporate-level, Defense enterprise software initiative when acquiring software. Officials indicated that most software will continue to be managed in a decentralized manner, with components continuing to be responsible for managing licenses for any software that is not purchased through an enterprise license agreement, but also stated there are plans to partially move to a more centralized approach.
Established comprehensive inventory	◑	According to Defense officials, software inventories have been completed for four of its components—the United States European Command, Defense Technology Security Administration, Defense Education Activity, and Defense Information Technology Center— and an inventory was provided for the European Command. In addition, Defense officials stated that inventories for the Air Force, Army, and Navy are expected to be completed by July 2014 and consolidated department-wide by the end of fiscal year 2014.
Regularly tracking and maintaining inventory using tools and metrics	◑	According to officials, the tracking, managing, and reporting of software licenses are completed by the components, as well as reconciliation of licenses, using a variety of methods and tools, both automated and manual. For example, for the European Command, Defense conducts quarterly software usage reports to monitor license usage on the network. However, it is unclear if department-wide automated tracking and managing is regularly occurring.
Analysis of software license data	∴	Defense has not analyzed the software license data to inform investment decisions. According to Defense's department-wide Selected Software Licenses Inventory Plan, the department plans to conduct analyses of the selected software license inventory when completed.
Sufficient training on software license management	◑	Defense has provided software license management training; however, it is unclear to what extent this training is available to appropriate personnel who are involved with managing software licenses. In particular, the training topics include components of software management (e.g., software asset management), end user license agreement negotiations, and support and maintenance.

Source: GAO analysis of Defense data.

Key:

● Fully met—the agency provided evidence that it fully addressed the leading practice.

◑ Partially met—the agency provided evidence that it addressed some, but not all, portions of the leading practice.

∴ Not met—the agency did not provide any evidence that it addressed the leading practice.

Department of Education

Table 7 provides a detailed summary of the results of our assessment of the Department of Education's (Education) practices for managing software licenses against leading practices.

Table 7: Assessment of Department of Education's Practices for Managing Software Licenses

Leading practice	GAO assessment	Summary of evidence
Develop comprehensive policy for management of software licenses	◑	Education has established a Handbook for Software Management and Acquisition Policy that generally includes centralized management, a software license inventory, tracking using automated tools, analysis, education and training, and goals and objectives. However, the handbook does not address life-cycle management. According to Education officials, the department plans to issue a replacement software license directive by early 2014 to allow the department to better centralize the management of its software licenses.
Centralized software license management approach	◑	Education's Office of the Chief Information Officer is responsible for establishing department procedures for software license management, according to officials. In addition, the department centrally manages 100 percent of its desktop software within its infrastructure environment through a contract. However, this contract does not span the management of all of the department's server-based software and software for systems managed separately by principal offices. According to Education officials, upon approval of a revised department directive, software license spending and licenses will be tracked in a more centralized manner.
Established comprehensive inventory	◑	Education has established a software license inventory through a contract. According to Education officials, the August 2013 workstation inventory provided to us represents the department's desktop software within its infrastructure environment, and the department does not have a centralized comprehensive inventory that represents 80 percent of the department's total software license spending and licenses. However, upon approval of a new directive, software licenses will be managed in a centralized manner.
Regularly tracking and maintaining inventory using tools and metrics	◑	Education does not regularly track and maintain comprehensive inventories of software licenses using automated tools and metrics. However, the department tracks and maintains workstation software license inventories monthly using an automated tool through a contract. According to Education officials, the department is unable to determine whether its workstation inventory represents at least 80 percent of its total software license spending or licenses since principal offices manage software outside of the contract.
Analysis of software license data	◑	Education has analyzed software requests for fiscal years 2012 and 2013 for new or updated software, according to officials. In addition, the department provided documentation illustrating its Enterprise Architecture Review Board's review of software being requested, including information on the number of Education staff that will use the software and how the software will be used in order to determine whether to make an investment. However, the department was not able to demonstrate that it has analyzed software license data department-wide, such as costs and trending data, to inform investment decisions to identify opportunities to reduce costs.
Sufficient training on software license management	◑	While Education has training on the appropriate use of software, it did not provide specific software license training on areas such as contract terms and conditions, laws, and regulations. For example, the agency's training specifies that all licensed software and documentation must be used in accordance with license agreements. According to officials, once the directive on managing software licenses is final, training to implement the guidance will occur.

Source: GAO analysis of Education data.

Key:

● Fully met—the agency provided evidence that it fully addressed the leading practice.

◑ Partially met—the agency provided evidence that it addressed some, but not all, portions of the leading practice.

:: Not met—the agency did not provide any evidence that it addressed the leading practice.

Department of Energy

Table 8 provides a detailed summary of the results of our assessment of the Department of Energy's (Energy) practices for managing software licenses against leading practices.

Table 8: Assessment of Department of Energy's Practices for Managing Software Licenses

Leading practice	GAO assessment	Summary of evidence
Develop comprehensive policy for management of software licenses	◑	Energy's policy, Order 200.1A on IT Management, requires the Office of the CIO to address centralized management through consolidation of software acquisition, volume purchasing arrangements and enterprise-wide agreements and track and maintain its inventory of software licenses. However, Energy does not have policy addressing analysis of license data to better inform investment decision making, education and training, establishing goals and objectives of the program, and managing licenses throughout their entire lifecycle.
Centralized software license management approach	◑	Energy's licenses are primarily managed in a decentralized manner. According to Energy officials, licenses within the Office of the Chief Information Officer are tracked centrally, which accounts for approximately 45 percent of the department's users.
Established comprehensive inventory	◑	Energy does have an inventory of software licenses; however, it is limited to the licenses managed by the Office of the Chief Information Officer, which, according to Energy officials, account for approximately 45 percent of the department's users. Specifically, this inventory includes information covering the version number, total number of licenses, and total number of licenses in use.
Regularly tracking and maintaining inventory using tools and metrics	◑	Energy uses automated tools to track licenses within the Office of the Chief Information Officer, but this only covers licenses managed by the office, which accounts for approximately 45 percent of department's users.
Analysis of software license data	::	Energy does not analyze the data to inform investment decisions and identify opportunities to reduce costs. Energy officials stated this is occurring at the program level; however, documentation to support this was not available.
Sufficient training on software license management	::	Energy has not provided relevant software license management training; however, according to officials, there may be localized training within programs and field sites.

Source: GAO analysis of Energy data.

Key:

● Fully met—the agency provided evidence that it fully addressed the leading practice.

◑ Partially met—the agency provided evidence that it addressed some, but not all, portions of the leading practice.

:: Not met—the agency did not provide any evidence that it addressed the leading practice.

Department of Health and Human Services

Table 9 provides a detailed summary of the results of our assessment of the Department of Health and Human Services' (HHS) practices for managing software licenses against leading practices.

Table 9: Assessment of Department of Health and Human Services' Practices for Managing Software Licenses

Leading practice	GAO assessment	Summary of evidence
Develop comprehensive policy for management of software licenses	∷	HHS officials stated that the department has not developed department-wide policies for managing software licenses. However, the officials stated that it has hired a Vendor Management Office Director and that the vendor management office will take the lead in centrally managing HHS commercial vendors and applicable software licenses. According to HHS officials, the establishment of the vendor management office is in process.
Centralized software license management approach	∷	While HHS officials stated it has a limited inventory, the department did not provide supporting documentation of this inventory. In addition, according to HHS officials, outside of a limited amount of information on software such as Windows and Microsoft Office, HHS manages its software licenses in a decentralized manner. HHS officials explained that the department's operating divisions manage their own needs and HHS does not have insight into the management of the majority of software or inventories. However, the department plans to fully staff a vendor management office to centralize the management of software licenses.
Established comprehensive inventory	∷	HHS has not established a comprehensive inventory representing the majority of software license spending or total licenses. According to officials, it does not have a comprehensive software license inventory because it has multiple operating divisions that internally manage software and software contracts do not clearly consist of just software.
Regularly tracking and maintaining inventory using tools and metrics	∷	HHS does not regularly track and maintain comprehensive inventories of software licenses using automated tools and metrics.
Analysis of software license data	∷	HHS has not analyzed fiscal year 2012 and 2013 department-wide software license data, such as costs, benefits, usage, and trending data, to inform investment decisions to identify opportunities to reduce costs. The department officials stated that this information is not available.
Sufficient training on software license management	∷	HHS officials stated that the department does not have documentation that it provided agency personnel with sufficient software license management training.

Source: GAO analysis of HHS data.

Key:

● Fully met—the agency provided evidence that it fully addressed the leading practice.

◐ Partially met—the agency provided evidence that it addressed some, but not all, portions of the leading practice.

∷ Not met—the agency did not provide any evidence that it addressed the leading practice.

Department of Homeland Security

Table 10 provides a detailed summary of the results of our assessment of the Department of Homeland Security's (DHS) practices for managing software licenses against leading practices.

Table 10: Assessment of Department of Homeland Security's Practices for Managing Software Licenses

Leading practice	GAO assessment	Summary of evidence
Develop comprehensive policy for management of software licenses	●	DHS has established policy that includes centralized management, establishing and tracking an inventory of software licenses, analysis of software data, education and training, goals and objectives, and life-cycle management.
Centralized software license management approach	◑	DHS's Office of the Chief Information Officer is responsible for managing enterprise license agreements and overall direction on software license management at the department level. However, execution of software license management occurs at the component level, according to DHS officials. These officials stated the enterprise licensing agreements do not represent the majority of the department's software license spending and it does not have a department-wide view of total licenses.
Established comprehensive inventory	◑	DHS's enterprise license agreement program office collects specific cost avoidance reports on the department's components, which DHS officials stated are provided by the appropriate vendors. However, DHS does not have a comprehensive inventory representing the majority of the department's software license spending and total licenses. According to DHS officials, components individually manage their usage data within the limits of enterprise agreement quantities and DHS does not develop or maintain that information.
Regularly tracking and maintaining inventory using tools and metrics	◑	DHS's enterprise license agreement program office collects software cost avoidance reports for DHS enterprise license agreements on agency components at least annually. However, according to DHS officials, the agency does not track comprehensive inventories using automated tools and metrics. DHS officials explained that agency components track software outside of DHS's enterprise license agreements and track their own inventory.
Analysis of software license data	◑	DHS has conducted business case assessments detailing historical spending and future trend data of select enterprise license agreements to inform investment decisions to identify opportunities to reduce costs. For example, DHS conducted department-wide contract business case assessments on recompeting for Adobe and Oracle enterprise license agreements. In addition, the department collects cost-avoidance reports for enterprise license agreements that have allowed DHS to make informed investment decisions. However, the department has not analyzed department-wide data such as costs, benefits, usage, and trending data outside of its enterprise license agreements to make cost-effective decisions, including decisions on what agency users need.
Sufficient training on software license management	◑	DHS has provided some training to personnel related to managing software licenses. For example, it has provided training on implementing internal controls to ensure that licenses are aligned with current user needs and are validated on a periodic basis. However, DHS did not demonstrate that it offers training in other important areas specific to software license management, such as contract terms and conditions, negotiations, security planning, or configuration management.

Source: GAO analysis of DHS data.

Key:

● Fully met—the agency provided evidence that it fully addressed the leading practice.

◑ Partially met—the agency provided evidence that it addressed some, but not all, portions of the leading practice.

∴ Not met—the agency did not provide any evidence that it addressed the leading practice.

Department of Housing and Urban Development

Table 11 provides a detailed summary of the results of our assessment of the Department of Housing and Urban Development's (HUD) practices for managing software licenses against leading practices.

Table 11: Assessment of Department of Housing and Urban Development's Practices for Managing Software Licenses

Leading practice	GAO assessment	Summary of evidence
Develop comprehensive policy for management of software licenses	◐	While HUD infrastructure requirements, including license management, are managed mostly through HUD's Information Technology Services contract, which has policies for management of those licenses, the agency has not established policy for the agency's licenses including Microsoft and Oracle, which account for about $7.2 million. HUD officials agreed that the agency's IT license management policies should be updated to reflect current licensing agreements for its software.
Centralized software license management approach	●	HUD manages software licenses in a centralized manner through its Office of the Chief Information Officer. HUD officials stated that about 95 percent of the software is managed through its infrastructure managed services contract. HUD oversees these contractor services through a set of service-level agreements that are tracked, monitored, and evaluated continuously by an independent verification and validation contract, according to officials. HUD officials also stated that its discovery tool licenses are managed by the HUD Office of the Chief Information Officer outside of its services contract.
Established comprehensive inventory	●	HUD oversees a comprehensive inventory of software the department uses. The majority of the software is managed by contractors. According to HUD officials, the Office of the Chief Information Officer oversees an inventory representing 95 percent of its software licenses, which are managed entirely by contractors through service-level agreements.
Regularly tracking and maintaining inventory using tools and metrics	◐	According to HUD officials, about 95 percent of the department's software, with the exception of discovery tool licenses, is managed by contractors that the Office of the Chief Information Officer oversees. HUD regularly tracks this software information through contractors and use of an automated tool. In addition, the department has acquired independent verification and validation contractor support to validate infrastructure service-level agreement metrics and performance information for all enterprise infrastructure services provided by contractors. However, HUD officials stated that the department's contracts do not have performance measures or service-level agreements specifically related to managing software licenses.
Analysis of software license data	○	HUD has not analyzed department-wide data, such as costs, benefits, usage, and trending data, to inform investment decisions to identify opportunities to reduce costs. According to HUD officials, the department's contractors provide enterprise infrastructure managed service requirements for supporting HUD's business and do not identify specific software licensing requirements. Accordingly, these officials stated that the department could not associate specific costs with software licenses provided by its contractors since contractors are providing a service at a fixed price. In addition, while HUD could provide cost information for software acquired outside of those contracts, it could not provide any related analysis of software data to inform its investment decisions.

Leading practice	GAO assessment	Summary of evidence
Sufficient training on software license management	∴	According to HUD officials, the department does not provide software license management training to agency personnel since contractors primarily manage software licenses under the oversight of the Office of the Chief Information Officer. However, no documentation was provided on training received by contactors to manage software licenses.

Source: GAO analysis of HUD data.

Key:

● Fully met—the agency provided evidence that it fully addressed the leading practice.

◐ Partially met—the agency provided evidence that it addressed some, but not all, portions of the leading practice.

∴ Not met—the agency did not provide any evidence that it addressed the leading practice.

Department of the Interior

Table 12 provides a detailed summary of the results of our assessment of the Department of the Interior's (Interior) practices for managing software licenses against leading practices.

Table 12: Assessment of Department of the Interior's Practices for Managing Software Licenses

Leading practice	GAO assessment	Summary of evidence
Develop comprehensive policy for management of software licenses	∴	Interior has not established comprehensive policy for management of software licenses.
Centralized software license management approach	∴	Interior's management of licenses is decentralized. Interior officials said that while the IT program itself is undergoing some centralization of duties and responsibilities, this will not include centralized management of software licenses.
Established comprehensive inventory	◐	Officials stated that the department does not have a comprehensive list of software licenses. While Interior provided an inventory of licenses managed by the Office of the Secretary, it is unclear if the inventory represents the majority of the department's licenses. Additionally, officials stated that some of the bureaus have specific inventories; however, documentation of these inventories was not provided.
Regularly tracking and maintaining inventory using tools and metrics	◐	Officials stated that they use an automated tool, but, do not regularly track, manage, and report on the majority of software licenses. Specifically, Interior is using Microsoft's System Center Configuration Manager to track 21 different applications and operating systems. In addition, according to department officials, Interior also uses spreadsheets to track licenses. However, the department is not frequently tracking, managing, and reporting on the majority of software licenses. According to officials, they only purchase what they need and that information is captured during the requirements-gathering phase of the acquisition. They also noted that with certain contracts, such as Microsoft, quarterly reporting is completed. In addition, officials noted that reports are not always provided via a spreadsheet and are at times provided through a management console specific to a vendor.

Leading practice	GAO assessment	Summary of evidence
Analysis of software license data	◐	According to Interior officials, the Office of the Chief Information Officer is required to review all IT acquisitions over a certain purchase limit and has analyzed the data trends to identify strategic sourcing opportunities. Specifically, Interior provided a business case template used by the department in conducting its oversight analyses that includes potential cost savings. For example, the analyses documented potential savings of $500,000 to $1 million in the first year, and subsequent annual savings of $100,000 for AutoDesk products. However, it is unclear whether these analyses are being informed by existing department-wide software license inventory data.
Sufficient training on software license management	∴	While Interior officials stated that the department provides training that addresses software licensing, copyrights, end user license agreements, and intellectual property laws, documentation was not available to support this.

Source: GAO analysis of Interior data.

Key:

● Fully met—the agency provided evidence that it fully addressed the leading practice.

◐ Partially met—the agency provided evidence that it addressed some, but not all, portions of the leading practice.

∴ Not met—the agency did not provide any evidence that it addressed the leading practice.

Department of Justice

Table 13 provides a detailed summary of the results of our assessment of the Department of Justice's (Justice) practices for managing software licenses against leading practices.

Table 13: Assessment of Department of Justice's Practices for Managing Software Licenses

Leading practice	GAO assessment	Summary of evidence
Develop comprehensive policy for management of software licenses	◐	Justice has a policy on governing the planning, acquisition, security, operation, management and use of IT resources that addresses centralized management. In particular, the policy states that for software purchases, Justice components shall use department enterprise license agreements, blanket purchase agreements, and other authorized contract vehicles, if economically advantageous. However, the policy does not specifically span the management of software licenses through establishing and tracking an inventory, analysis, education and training, goals and objectives, and life-cycle management.
Centralized software license management approach	◐	Justice's Office of the Chief Information Officer centrally manages enterprise-wide solutions and services, such as Oracle, Adobe, and Microsoft agreements. However, Justice officials stated that components are not required to use or buy software using these agreements, but they almost always do. According to Justice officials, there is no process to manage all software licenses department-wide and management of IT resources occurs primarily at the component level. To better address centralized management, Justice officials stated that the department plans to develop a vendor management program office and define new related processes in the third and fourth quarters of fiscal year 2014.

Leading practice	GAO assessment	Summary of evidence
Established comprehensive inventory	◖	Justice has centralized inventory information for Oracle, Adobe, and Microsoft enterprise license agreements. However, it does not have a comprehensive inventory representing the majority of software licenses used across the department and the majority of its total software license spending. According to officials, management of IT resources is performed primarily at the component level.
Regularly tracking and maintaining inventory using tools and metrics	◖	Justice annually tracks and manages centralized enterprise license agreement information for products such as Microsoft and Oracle within the Office of Chief Information Officer. However, officials stated that these software data may not capture all of its components' procured software since these enterprise license agreements are not mandatory and the department does not have an automated tool that incorporates software license management-specific metrics.
Analysis of software license data	∷	Justice was unable to provide documentation showing that it analyzed software license data department-wide, such as costs, benefits, usage, and trending data, to inform investment decisions and identify opportunities to reduce costs.
Sufficient training on software license management	∷	While Justice officials stated that personnel have participated in relevant training such as acquisition workshops, the agency was unable to provide documentation of training and stated it does not have a software license management training program.

Source: GAO analysis of Justice data.

Key:

● Fully met—the agency provided evidence that it fully addressed the leading practice.

◖ Partially met—the agency provided evidence that it addressed some, but not all, portions of the leading practice.

∷ Not met—the agency did not provide any evidence that it addressed the leading practice.

Department of Labor

Table 14 provides a detailed summary of the results of our assessment of the Department of Labor's (Labor) practices for managing software licenses against leading practices.

Table 14: Assessment of Department of Labor's Practices for Managing Software Licenses

Leading practice	GAO assessment	Summary of evidence
Develop comprehensive policy for management of software licenses	●	Labor has developed comprehensive policies for the management of software licenses. For example, the Labor software license management process establishes, among other things, how the department manages installation requests and licensing of software that is applicable to the Office of the Chief Information Officer and its customers, and how licenses become part of the inventory.
Centralized software license management approach	◖	Labor has a process to manage all of its Microsoft enterprise license agreements, and other software managed within the Office of the Chief Information Officer. However, Labor officials stated that it does not track software licenses of its components. To address this weakness, officials stated that the department is currently consolidating IT infrastructure services for nine components into the Office of the Chief Information Officer and this effort is expected to be complete in fiscal year 2016.

Leading practice	GAO assessment	Summary of evidence
Established comprehensive inventory	◐	Labor has an inventory managed by its Office of the Chief Information Officer. However, this inventory does not represent the majority of the departmental components' software licenses and software license spending department-wide.
Regularly tracking and maintaining inventory using tools and metrics	◐	Labor tracks inventory reports using an automated tool that tracks licenses in real-time and stated these reports are generated annually, when software licenses are up for renewal. However, Labor officials stated the inventory only includes the software managed by the Office of the Chief Information Officer. In addition, officials stated no additional metrics exist outside of the inventory report's software counts, and its tool does not track spending data.
Analysis of software license data	∴	While Labor provided documentation of the agency's software consolidation efforts, the documentation did not illustrate that Labor conducted an analysis on department-wide software license data, such as costs, benefits, usage, and trending data, to inform investment decisions to identify opportunities to reduce costs.
Sufficient training on software license management	∴	According to Labor officials, the department has not provided appropriate personnel with sufficient software license management training.

Source: GAO analysis of Labor data.

Key:

● Fully met—the agency provided evidence that it fully addressed the leading practice.

◐ Partially met—the agency provided evidence that it addressed some, but not all, portions of the leading practice.

∴ Not met—the agency did not provide any evidence that it addressed the leading practice.

Department of State

Table 15 provides a detailed summary of the results of our assessment of the Department of State's (State) practices for managing software licenses against leading practices.

Table 15: Assessment of Department of State's Practices for Managing Software Licenses

Leading practice	GAO assessment	Summary of evidence
Develop comprehensive policy for management of software licenses	◐	State has policies which govern the centralized management of software licenses and tracking software licenses. Specifically, the Bureau of Information Resource Management policy identifies responsibilities for the management of Microsoft and Oracle enterprise license agreements and the tracking of software licenses. However, there are no policies addressing establishing a comprehensive inventory, analyses of software license data, training on management of software licenses, goals and objectives, and consideration of the software license life-cycle phases.
Centralized software license management approach	◐	According to State officials, enterprise agreements are managed centrally, while the remaining licenses are managed on a bureau-by-bureau basis. Specifically, Microsoft and Oracle enterprise license agreements are managed centrally, and VMware and Adobe have blanket purchase agreements that have cross-bureau participation within the department, which are also managed centrally. Officials noted that the department has established an Enterprise Licensing Steering Committee that plans to create more efficiency through centralization.

Leading practice	GAO assessment	Summary of evidence
Established comprehensive inventory	◒	While the department has an inventory of software applications, including Microsoft licenses, it is not comprehensive. According to State officials, the department is working on establishing a department-wide inventory that will include Oracle, Symantec, and Entrust, but a timeline for implementation is not yet determined.
Regularly tracking and maintaining inventory using tools and metrics	◒	While the department is centrally tracking Microsoft licenses using automated tools, other licenses such as Oracle, Symantec, and Entrust are not being tracked. According to officials, as the tool evolves, State plans to automate many of the reconciliation processes and metrics it uses. In addition, it is unclear at what interval reporting is occurring.
Analysis of software license data	◒	While State has conducted analysis using its automated tracking tool, including an analysis of license costs and quantity by location, there is limited evidence showing how it is used to inform investment decision making. State officials said the department plans to begin analyzing software license data to inform investment decisions, but did not provide a time frame for implementation.
Sufficient training on software license management	∴	State has not provided software license management training to employees, but stated that its newly established steering committee is focused on software licenses and will take training into consideration.

Source: GAO analysis of State data.

Key:

● Fully met—the agency provided evidence that it fully addressed the leading practice.

◒ Partially met—the agency provided evidence that it addressed some, but not all, portions of the leading practice.

∴ Not met—the agency did not provide any evidence that it addressed the leading practice.

Department of Transportation

Table 16 provides a detailed summary of the results of our assessment of the Department of Transportation's (DOT) practices for managing software licenses against leading practices.

Table 16: Assessment of Department of Transportation's Practices for Managing Software Licenses

Leading practice	GAO assessment	Summary of evidence
Develop comprehensive policy for management of software licenses	◒	DOT has a policy addressing components of centralized management and management of software licenses through the entire life cycle. According to officials, DOT is in the process of updating its policy; however, it is unclear if this update will address establishing an inventory of licenses, regularly tracking licenses using automated tools, analyzing license data to inform investment decision making, providing license management training to personnel, and establishing goals and objectives of the program. DOT officials expect to have this policy in place by December 2014.

Leading practice	GAO assessment	Summary of evidence
Centralized software license management approach	◑	DOT manages most of its licenses through a common operating environment deployed to each DOT workstation. However, this does not include software within the Federal Aviation Administration or specialized software. Specifically, according to DOT officials, this accounts for approximately 94 percent of the users within the department (11,177 out of 11,799 users). Officials noted that the 11,799 users do not include any of the users from the Federal Aviation Administration, and DOT is uncertain how many users are within this component.
Established comprehensive inventory	◑	DOT provided an inventory for its common operating environment, but not a department-wide inventory. According to officials, this accounts for approximately 94 percent of the users within DOT, not including users from the Federal Aviation Administration.
Regularly tracking and maintaining inventory using tools and metrics	◑	DOT tracks and maintains all licenses within the common operating environment on a monthly basis. Specifically, reports are run using automated tools, specifically Microsoft's System Center Configuration Manager, Safeboot Management Console, and Stratusphere. However, the department does not track or maintain comprehensive inventories within the Federal Aviation Administration.
Analysis of software license data	◑	While DOT conducted analyses for Microsoft products in 2012 and 2013, it is unclear to what extent the department has done so for other licenses. DOT officials stated that it is conducting analysis as contracts expire. Specifically, this process includes a comparison of current needs with the previous year's count and occurs during contract renewals. Additionally, according to officials, a survey was conducted last year that resulted in a reduction of Acrobat Pro licenses, but documentation to support this analysis was not available.
Sufficient training on software license management	∴	DOT has not provided software license management training to its employees and it does not have plans to do so, according to officials.

Source: GAO analysis of DOT data.

Key:

● Fully met—the agency provided evidence that it fully addressed the leading practice.

◑ Partially met—the agency provided evidence that it addressed some, but not all, portions of the leading practice.

∴ Not met—the agency did not provide any evidence that it addressed the leading practice.

Department of the Treasury

Table 17 provides a detailed summary of the results of our assessment of the Department of the Treasury's (Treasury) practices for managing software licenses against leading practices.

Table 17: Assessment of Department of the Treasury's Practices for Managing Software Licenses

Leading practice	GAO assessment	Summary of evidence
Develop comprehensive policy for management of software licenses	◑	Treasury has policies in place addressing the establishment of a comprehensive inventory of software licenses and the analysis of data to inform investment decisions and identify opportunities to reduce costs. However, policies and procedures addressing centralized management, tracking licenses regularly using automated tools, providing software license management education and training to personnel, establishing goals and objectives for the program, and managing licenses throughout their entire life cycle do not exist.
Centralized software license management approach	⸪	Treasury manages licenses in a decentralized manner. Specifically, while Treasury does pursue enterprise software license agreements across the department as part of strategic sourcing, the agreements leave the management of these licenses to the bureaus.
Established comprehensive inventory	◑	According to officials, Treasury does not have a consolidated inventory because the process of managing software licenses occurs at the individual bureaus. However, Treasury did provide an inventory of software licenses from April to June 2013, which was established using an automated tool. The inventory includes counts of licenses for specific applications. According to Treasury officials, the tool collects data on all devices connected to the Treasury network at any given time.
Regularly tracking and maintaining inventory using tools and metrics	◑	The department performs monthly scans of software using an automated tool that looks at hardware, software, usage, number of licenses, and number of licenses installed, but according to officials, the tracking of these licenses using automated tools occurs at the bureau-level and tracking is not conducted department-wide.
Analysis of software license data	⸪	The department does not exclusively track whether specific software license data have been used to inform investment decisions.
Sufficient training on software license management	⸪	Treasury's Office of the Chief Information Officer does not provide software license management training to its employees.

Source: GAO analysis of Treasury data.

Key:

● Fully met—the agency provided evidence that it fully addressed the leading practice.

◑ Partially met—the agency provided evidence that it addressed some, but not all, portions of the leading practice.

⸪ Not met—the agency did not provide any evidence that it addressed the leading practice.

Department of Veterans Affairs

Table 18 provides a detailed summary of the results of our assessment of the Department of Veterans Affairs' (VA) practices for managing software licenses against leading practices.

Table 18: Assessment of Department of Veterans Affairs' Practices for Managing Software Licenses

Leading practice	GAO assessment	Summary of evidence
Develop comprehensive policy for management of software licenses	◑	VA has a policy on centralized management of licenses, which includes goals and objectives of a software license management program. In addition, a draft policy addresses establishing an inventory, tracking using tools, and using analysis to better inform investment decision making. Officials stated they are uncertain when it will be finalized.
Centralized software license management approach	◑	VA centrally manages the software licenses that are procured through an enterprise license agreement. In addition, officials stated they are planning to move toward a more centralized approach to managing the majority of its software licenses, but no time frame for completion was provided. Specifically, VA has established a Technology Innovation Program Office to enhance its capabilities to manage software as an asset.
Established comprehensive inventory	◑	While VA provided an inventory of licenses, it is not comprehensive. VA officials stated that a comprehensive inventory will be achieved over time as the policies and procedures for the Technology Innovation Program Office are established and enforced.
Regularly tracking and maintaining inventory using tools and metrics	◑	VA uses automated tools to track software that accounts for some data and manually tracks information on how many licenses VA owns or is entitled to operate. However, according to officials, the Technology Innovation Program Office is investigating the best methods for compiling an inventory of licenses.
Analysis of software license data	◑	While VA has analyzed data on its Microsoft enterprise licenses, it has not done so for other software licenses. Specifically, in 2012, VA conducted an analysis of Microsoft license data that resulted in a reported savings of over $30 million. This was attributed to a recompetition which resulted in all software under this agreement being aggregated as one purchase. However, officials stated they are unclear if this type of analysis is performed on all enterprise license agreements. VA officials stated one of the goals of the Technology Innovation Program Office is to ensure this type of analysis is performed for all future license purchases.
Sufficient training on software license management	∴	VA officials indicated that training has been completed through a contract with Gartner. However, the department did not provide documentation to support that this training has occurred.

Source: GAO analysis of VA data.

Key:

● Fully met—the agency provided evidence that it fully addressed the leading practice.

◑ Partially met—the agency provided evidence that it addressed some, but not all, portions of the leading practice.

∴ Not met—the agency did not provide any evidence that it addressed the leading practice.

Environmental Protection Agency

Table 19 provides a detailed summary of the results of our assessment of the Environmental Protection Agency's (EPA) practices for managing software licenses against leading practices.

Table 19: Assessment of Environmental Protection Agency's Practices for Managing Software Licenses

Leading practice	GAO assessment	Summary of evidence
Develop comprehensive policy for management of software licenses	◑	EPA has policies which address inventories and tracking software licenses using tools at the business unit level, but not at the agency-wide level. For example, EPA's Software Management and Piracy policy states that license management is decentralized and that inventories are to be established and maintained through tracking by each individual program office. EPA does not have policies for centralized management of licenses, analysis to inform decision making, education and training, goals of the program, and management throughout the entire life cycle. According to officials, further development of comprehensive software license management policies is planned; however, no time frame for completion was provided.
Centralized software license management approach	∷	EPA's management of software licenses is decentralized and there are no plans to move it to a centralized approach. Specifically, while licenses may be managed centrally within a business unit, this is not managed at the departmental level.
Established comprehensive inventory	◑	While EPA provided an inventory for a portion of licenses managed by one business unit, its Office of Technology and Operations, it is incomplete. Specifically, the inventory includes information on cost per unit and number of licenses for some but not all applications. Additionally, officials stated that it does not have a comprehensive inventory of licenses within EPA and they are uncertain if inventories exist for its other business units.
Regularly tracking and maintaining inventory using tools and metrics	∷	EPA does not regularly track and maintain comprehensive inventories of software licenses using automated tools and metrics. Officials said the Office of Technology and Operations uses spreadsheets to manually manage enterprise software licenses, but the inventory was incomplete.
Analysis of software license data	∷	EPA is not analyzing data to inform investment decisions and identify opportunities to reduce costs. Officials attributed this to software not being considered an investment in the same terms as a traditional investment that would undergo capital planning and investment control review.
Sufficient training on software license management	∷	EPA has not provided training in software license management.

Source: GAO analysis of EPA data.

Key:

● Fully met—the agency provided evidence that it fully addressed the leading practice.

◑ Partially met—the agency provided evidence that it addressed some, but not all, portions of the leading practice.

∷ Not met—the agency did not provide any evidence that it addressed the leading practice.

General Services Administration

Table 20 provides a detailed summary of the results of our assessment of the General Services Administration's (GSA) practices for managing software licenses against leading practices.

Table 20: Assessment of General Services Administration's Practices for Managing Software Licenses

Leading practice	GAO assessment	Summary of evidence
Develop comprehensive policy for management of software licenses	◐	GSA has documented guidelines and processes for managing software licenses generally, such as its contract standard operating procedures for software requests and deployment. These procedures span tracking software license data through use of an automated tool and database. However, the agency's policies do not include other leading practices, including a centralized management approach, analysis, education and training, goals and objectives, and life-cycle management for all of the agency's software licenses. According to GSA officials, to address these issues, it is in the process of centralizing its efforts through consolidating the agency's IT departments into a single unit under the direction of the Chief Information Officer and plans to develop revised policies during fiscal year 2014.
Centralized software license management approach	●	GSA centrally manages software licenses for the majority of software licenses. Specifically, the server-based and enterprise-wide licenses are managed centrally, whereas non-enterprise-wide workstation software licenses are generally managed regionally.
Established comprehensive inventory	◐	GSA has a comprehensive centralized inventory representing at least 88 percent of the agency's total software license spending. However, the agency was not able to show that it incorporated automated discovery and inventory tools that provide easy search and access to software license information, such as contract terms and agreement records.
Regularly tracking and maintaining inventory using tools and metrics	◐	GSA tracks an inventory using a reporting validation tool and stated it periodically tracks existing software data within its software asset management system. The agency was able to provide a copy of its centralized inventory as of October 2013 and illustrate reporting validation capabilities. However, the agency officials stated prior-year inventory information is generally not available since GSA has just recently transitioned to a larger GSA IT enterprise as part of its consolidation efforts.
Analysis of software license data	◐	GSA officials stated that the agency has evaluated tools and technologies through comparison of selected product cost and benefit data to inform investment decisions to identify opportunities to reduce costs. While GSA was able to provide supporting documentation of its analysis of costs and benefits of selected products, the agency could not show that it has analyzed agency-wide software license data, such as costs, benefits, usage, and trending data, to inform investment decisions and identify opportunities to reduce costs.
Sufficient training on software license management	∷	GSA has not provided software license management training and education to appropriate agency personnel. However, GSA officials stated it has plans to develop software asset life-cycle management training through an organized team once the IT reorganization is complete.

Source: GAO analysis of GSA data.

Key:

● Fully met—the agency provided evidence that it fully addressed the leading practice.

◐ Partially met—the agency provided evidence that it addressed some, but not all, portions of the leading practice.

∷ Not met—the agency did not provide any evidence that it addressed the leading practice.

National Aeronautics and Space Administration

Table 21 provides a detailed summary of the results of our assessment of the National Aeronautics and Space Administration's (NASA) practices for managing software licenses against leading practices.

Table 21: Assessment of National Aeronautics and Space Administration's Practices for Managing Software Licenses

Leading practice	GAO assessment	Summary of evidence
Develop comprehensive policy for management of software licenses	◑	NASA has established relevant agency-wide software license management policies, such as its November 2012 Shared Services Delivery Guide and Procurement notice 04-75, which discusses the use of the Enterprise License Management Team. This policy covers centralized management, establishing an inventory, tracking using automated tools, analysis, and goals and objectives. However, this policy does not address life-cycle management and education and training.
Centralized software license management approach	◑	NASA manages some software licenses in a centralized manner through use of the agency's enterprise license management team program. However, other software is managed within other program areas, such as the solutions for enterprise-wide procurement and the IT infrastructure integration program. For example, the enterprise license management team program provides the Office of Chief Information Officer support for, among other things, the analysis and review of its enterprise licensing.
Established comprehensive inventory	◑	NASA has established a software license inventory through its enterprise license management team. However, this inventory does not represent the majority of the agency's total licenses and spending.
Regularly tracking and maintaining inventory using tools and metrics	◑	NASA tracks information within the agency's enterprise license management team database using an automated tool and reports on this information at least annually. However, agency officials stated it does not track the software for the other program areas such as NASA's solutions for enterprise-wide procurement.
Analysis of software license data	◑	While NASA's enterprise license management team has developed software license business cases to inform investment decisions to identify opportunities to reduce cost, the agency has not done so for other software licenses that represent the majority of licenses. For example, the enterprise license management team developed a business case on selected software, examined benefits and costs, and recommended the establishment of an agency-wide blanket purchase agreement to provide NASA space centers with lower cost, reduced administrative effort, and simplified contract renewal, among other things. NASA officials also stated that in fiscal year 2013 the agency realized $32.7 million in cost savings through its IT infrastructure integration program. However, NASA has not analyzed agency-wide data, such as costs, benefits, usage, and trending data, for all of its software licenses to make cost-effective decisions, including decisions about what users need.
Sufficient training on software license management	◑	NASA has developed relevant training on software license management and provided an April 2013 webinar to all procurement offices across the agency. This webinar presentation included information on the program's mission, objectives, members, dependencies and interfaces, and business cases. However, this training did not include aspects of sufficient software license management training such as negotiations, laws and regulations, and contract terms and conditions agency-wide.

Source: GAO analysis of NASA data.

Key:

● Fully met—the agency provided evidence that it fully addressed the leading practice.

◑ Partially met—the agency provided evidence that it addressed some, but not all, portions of the leading practice.

.·. Not met—the agency did not provide any evidence that it addressed the leading practice.

National Science Foundation

Table 22 provides a detailed summary of the results of our assessment of the National Science Foundation's (NSF) practices for managing software licenses against leading practices.

Table 22: Assessment of National Science Foundation's Practices for Managing Software Licenses

Leading practice	GAO assessment	Summary of evidence
Develop comprehensive policy for management of software licenses	.·.	While NSF officials described several components of software license management in use, these practices are not documented in policies.
Centralized software license management approach	●	NSF has a centralized approach for managing licenses. Specifically, licenses are managed centrally through NSF's Division of Information Systems, which accounts for the majority of software licenses. Management of licenses for special-use software is decentralized, but special-use software accounts for a small portion of NSF's overall software inventory.
Established comprehensive inventory	●	NSF has a comprehensive inventory of software licenses. For example, licenses for desktop products are managed either through an enterprise-wide agreement with the vendor or through the agency's application management and deployment tool. Additionally, for non-desktop software, the management of licenses is available through the product vendor, or manually tracked.
Regularly tracking and maintaining inventory using tools and metrics	◐	While NSF uses automated tools to track software licenses, it does not do so on a regular basis. Specifically, management of the Microsoft enterprise licenses is facilitated by automated reporting, and includes annual license reconciliation. Other enterprise-wide office productivity software is managed through an application management and deployment tool, which provides reporting on software utilization and facilitates installation of approved software based on available licensing. Although officials stated this is done on an annual basis, no documentation was available to support this.
Analysis of software license data	◐	While NSF has analyzed data on its Microsoft licenses to inform investment decisions at the time of renewal, it has not done so for other licenses. For example, NSF provided documentation of annual license reconciliation for Microsoft products, which consists of a spreadsheet used to reconcile the number of Microsoft licenses per product (as obtained through the Microsoft portal). It details the final count based upon analysis of the number of licenses needed for the renewal.
Sufficient training on software license management	.·.	NSF does not provide training related to software license management. Officials attributed this to not having designated software license management professionals within the agency.

Source: GAO analysis of NSF data.

Key:

● Fully met—the agency provided evidence that it fully addressed the leading practice.

◐ Partially met—the agency provided evidence that it addressed some, but not all, portions of the leading practice.

∴ Not met—the agency did not provide any evidence that it addressed the leading practice.

Nuclear Regulatory Commission

Table 23 provides a detailed summary of the results of our assessment of the Nuclear Regulatory Commission's (NRC) practices for managing software licenses against leading practices.

Table 23: Assessment of Nuclear Regulatory Commission's Practices for Managing Software Licenses

Leading practice	GAO assessment	Summary of evidence
Develop comprehensive policy for management of software licenses	◖	NRC has policies in place addressing centralized management of software licenses, the development of a comprehensive inventory of licenses, the use of appropriate tools to track licenses, analysis, goals and objectives of managing software licenses, and some phases of managing through the entire software licenses management life cycle. However, it does not have a policy addressing education and training.
Centralized software license management approach	◖	NRC has implemented some centralized activities through its contractor. Specifically, the contractor is responsible for establishing the inventory of software licenses, tracking and maintaining licenses using automated discovery tools, and analyzing license data. However, officials stated that various offices within NRC also have responsibility for software license management activities. According to officials, there are plans to move to a more centralized model; however, a time frame for implementation was not provided.
Established comprehensive inventory	◖	NRC has several inventories of software licenses, but they are not comprehensive. For example, NRC provided an inventory by program office tracking the estimated number of users; an inventory of applications (names only) within the agency's Dell Information Technology and Infrastructure Support Services contract; inventory of licenses used by NRC's Operations Center Information Management System; two inventories of licenses used by NRC's Office of Nuclear Regulatory Research; and RES software. In addition, NRC does not have documentation regarding the process used to validate and ensure the accuracy and reliability of the inventories.
Regularly tracking and maintaining inventory using tools and metrics	◖	NRC primarily conducts tracking, management, and reporting of software license information using both automated (through the use of Remedy ARS) and manual data entry and reconciliation into Excel spreadsheets and Microsoft Access databases. However, while officials stated the contractor is conducting tracking on a quarterly basis, NRC did not provide documentation of this occurrence.
Analysis of software license data	◖	While NRC has conducted analysis for its Microsoft Project and Visio licenses, officials stated they are uncertain if this analysis is occurring for the majority of its software licenses.
Sufficient training on software license management	◖	NRC has provided some software license management training to employees. For example, the agency has provided training in areas related to configuration management. However, training has not been provided in the areas of contract terms and conditions or negotiations.

Source: GAO analysis of NRC data.

Key:

● Fully met—the agency provided evidence that it fully addressed the leading practice.

◖ Partially met—the agency provided evidence that it addressed some, but not all, portions of the leading practice.

∴ Not met—the agency did not provide any evidence that it addressed the leading practice.

Office of Personnel Management

Table 24 provides a detailed summary of the results of our assessment of the Office of Personnel Management's (OPM) practices for managing software licenses against leading practices.

Table 24: Assessment of Office of Personnel Management's Practices for Managing Software Licenses

Leading practice	GAO assessment	Summary of evidence
Develop comprehensive policy for management of software licenses	◐	While OPM has developed a policy relevant to managing software licenses, it has not established how to implement the policy. For example, its July 2009 policy on IT procurement and its April 2013 OPM System Development Life Cycle Policy and Standards combined include centralized management, establishing and tracking an inventory, analysis, education and training, goals and objectives, and life cycle management.
Centralized software license management approach	◐	OPM manages its software licenses in a partially centralized manner. The agency manages its enterprise license agreements through the Office of the Chief Information Officer. However, the agency officials stated that outside of enterprise license agreements, the Office of the Chief Information Officer does not have visibility into program office software license spending.
Established comprehensive inventory	◐	The OPM Office of the Chief Information Officer has established an inventory of the agency's enterprise license agreements through multiple spreadsheets. However, agency officials stated that these spreadsheets do not represent a comprehensive agency-wide software license inventory. These officials explained that software purchased from program offices outside of Office of the Chief Information Officer enterprise license agreements are not actively captured through an inventory. However, according to officials, the percentage of software license spending the Office of the Chief Information Officer has visibility into was less than 65 percent for fiscal years 2012 and 2013.
Regularly tracking and maintaining inventory using tools and metrics	◐	The agency's Office of the Chief Information Officer annually tracks and maintains an inventory of enterprise license agreement software using multiple spreadsheets that are primarily tracked manually and include software counts. In addition, one inventory is partially managed through the use of an automated tool, and multiple inventories have established metrics such as processor usage.
Analysis of software license data	◐	While OPM has conducted analysis of its Microsoft enterprise license agreements for fiscal year 2013, it has not analyzed agency-wide data for other licenses. Specifically, to determine whether OPM should renew its Microsoft enterprise license agreement for fiscal year 2013, the agency's investment review board reviewed its historical and anticipated future maintenance cost information and the agency's analysis of cost savings. Based on this analysis, the agency determined that not renewing the Microsoft enterprise licensing agreement would cost it, at a minimum, an additional 7 percent, or $182,000, increase in maintenance costs. However, OPM could not illustrate that it analyzed agency-wide software license data, such as costs, benefits, usage, and trending data, to inform investment decisions since it does not have a comprehensive software license inventory.
Sufficient training on software license management	◌	While OPM officials stated it has briefed staff on topics such as enterprise license agreements and the executive order on computer software piracy, the officials stated that no software license management education and training documentation exists.

Source: GAO analysis of OPM data.

Key:

● Fully met—the agency provided evidence that it fully addressed the leading practice.

◐ Partially met—the agency provided evidence that it addressed some, but not all, portions of the leading practice.

∴ Not met—the agency did not provide any evidence that it addressed the leading practice.

Small Business Administration

Table 25 provides a detailed summary of the results of our assessment of the Small Business Administration's (SBA) practices for managing software licenses against leading practices.

Table 25: Assessment of Small Business Administration's Practices for Managing Software Licenses

Leading practice	GAO assessment	Summary of evidence
Develop comprehensive policy for management of software licenses	◐	SBA has policies on maintaining an inventory and establishing goals and objectives; however, SBA officials stated the agency does not have any standard operating procedures or a general policy to manage all software licenses agency-wide. Specifically, SBA's information notice on rules governing the use of Microsoft software from 2003 has guidance to ensure compliance with SBA's licensing agreement with Microsoft, but it does not span use of software agency-wide.
Centralized software license management approach	◐	SBA manages its software licenses in a partially centralized manner. According to officials, the Office of the Chief Information Officer centrally manages standard desktop and network-based software titles. However, agency officials stated that it does not track software licenses from several program offices outside of the Office of the CIO.
Established comprehensive inventory	◐	SBA has an inventory, but it is not comprehensive. The agency was unable to determine the percentage of total software licenses and software license spending it manages centrally through an inventory since the data exclude information from several program offices. However, according to SBA officials, the agency has a tool to discover all software licenses on its network, which is expected to be functional and deployed in fiscal year 2014. As of November 2013, the tool had not been deployed.
Regularly tracking and maintaining inventory using tools and metrics	∴	SBA was not able to illustrate that it regularly tracks and maintains an inventory of software licenses using automated tools and metrics. To address this challenge of not tracking agency-wide data, SBA officials stated SBA expects to deploy a functional discovery tool that will track software licenses agency-wide and incorporate related metrics in fiscal year 2014.
Analysis of software license data	∴	SBA did not have documentation showing that it has analyzed agency-wide software license data to inform investment decisions and identify opportunities to reduce costs.
Sufficient training on software license management	∴	SBA has not provided appropriate agency personnel with sufficient software license management training.

Source: GAO analysis of SBA data.

Key:

● Fully met—the agency provided evidence that it fully addressed the leading practice.

◐ Partially met—the agency provided evidence that it addressed some, but not all, portions of the leading practice.

∴ Not met—the agency did not provide any evidence that it addressed the leading practice.

Social Security Administration

Table 26 provides a detailed summary of the results of our assessment of the Social Security Administration's (SSA) practices for managing software licenses against leading practices.

Table 26: Assessment of Social Security Administration's Practices for Managing Software Licenses

Leading practice	GAO assessment	Summary of evidence
Develop comprehensive policy for management of software licenses	◐	SSA has policies describing the agency's roles and responsibilities, and objectives relevant to software license management. However, it does not have policies for identifying and collecting information about software license agreements using automated discovery and inventory tools incorporating metrics, regularly tracking and maintaining software licenses, analysis of software usage and other data, providing training relevant to software license management; and consideration of the software license management life-cycle phases.
Centralized software license management approach	◐	SSA centrally manages a small percentage of the agency's total licenses and license spending through its Enterprise Software Engineering Tools Board inventory. SSA officials stated that it manages mainframe and Microsoft desktop software centrally. However, the officials stated that the agency has delegated the responsibility of software license management to component local managers and, as a result, does not centrally manage the majority of the agency's software licenses.
Established comprehensive inventory	◐	The agency has established an inventory through its Enterprise Software Engineering Tools Board. However, according to officials, this inventory is representative of a small percentage of the agency's total software license spending and total licenses. In addition, while the agency officials stated that it centrally manages Microsoft licenses and maintenance software, it did not have documentation of any inventory. Overall, SSA officials stated that it does not have a comprehensive inventory representing the majority of its software license spending and total licenses. However, agency officials stated the agency plans to implement a software asset management system to better establish a comprehensive inventory.
Regularly tracking and maintaining inventory using tools and metrics	◐	SSA uses a support tool to track a small percentage of the agency's total software licenses. However, officials stated that it has no established time frames for reporting on the tool. According to agency officials, since SSA is not fully centralized, the agency does not track comprehensive inventories using automated tools and metrics. To better centralize all of its software licenses, agency officials stated it plans to implement a software asset management system.
Analysis of software license data	◐	While SSA has analyzed selected software license data, the agency has not analyzed department-wide software license data to inform investment decisions and identify opportunities to reduce costs. According to SSA officials, the agency analyzes software license data on a contract-by-contract basis to inform investment decisions and identify opportunities to reduce costs. The officials stated that it has reduced ongoing costs of large mainframe contracts as a result of the process. SSA has specifically worked with an independent licensing vendor to analyze the agency's mainframe usage and portfolio to assist the agency in contract negotiations. In January 2012, the vendor conducted a renewal mainframe analysis where it identified mainframe pricing considerations for SSA. However, outside of the mainframe contracts, SSA was not able to demonstrate that it analyzes software license data agency-wide, such as costs, benefits, usage, and trending data, to inform investment decisions and identify opportunities to reduce costs.

Leading practice	GAO assessment	Summary of evidence
Sufficient training on software license management	∴	SSA has not provided appropriate agency personnel with sufficient software license management training.

Source: GAO analysis of SSA data.

Key:

● Fully met—the agency provided evidence that it fully addressed the leading practice.

◐ Partially met—the agency provided evidence that it addressed some, but not all, portions of the leading practice.

∴ Not met—the agency did not provide any evidence that it addressed the leading practice.

U.S. Agency for International Development

Table 27 provides a detailed summary of the results of our assessment of the U.S. Agency for International Development's (USAID) practices for managing software licenses against leading practices.

Table 27: Assessment of U.S. Agency for International Development's Practices for Managing Software Licenses

Leading practice	GAO assessment	Summary of evidence
Develop comprehensive policy for management of software license	◐	USAID's policy, ADS 547, and its standard operating procedure for a contract with IBM address centralized management, the establishment of a comprehensive inventory, goals and objectives of the software license management program, and the management of licenses throughout the entire life cycle. Officials stated there are plans to conduct analysis to monitor software usage; however, no time frame for implementation was provided. In addition, policies and procedures for tracking software using automated tools and education and training do not exist.
Centralized software license management approach	●	USAID has a contract in place with IBM for centrally managing licenses for all of USAID's operating units.
Established comprehensive inventory	◐	While USAID maintains an inventory of licenses through a contractor, there is no established, documented process for validating and ensuring the accuracy and reliability of the data provided by the contractor. USAID provided an inventory from April 2013 of licenses installed at headquarters and on each mission's servers. USAID estimates that as of January 2014, this accounted for approximately 95 percent of its software licenses.
Regularly tracking and maintaining inventory using tools and metrics	◐	USAID is using an automated tool, specifically Microsoft's System Center Configuration Manager, to track and manage software licenses for Microsoft products on an annual basis. However, officials are uncertain how other applications are being tracked and maintained.
Analysis of software license data	◐	USAID officials stated that analysis is conducted on an ad-hoc basis. While the agency provided documentation of such analysis capabilities, it did not describe how it was used to inform investment decision making.
Sufficient training on software license management	∴	USAID officials stated that its contractor's employees receive software license management training, but no documentation was available.

Source: GAO analysis of USAID data.

Key:

● Fully met—the agency provided evidence that it fully addressed the leading practice.

◐ Partially met—the agency provided evidence that it addressed some, but not all, portions of the leading practice.

∴ Not met—the agency did not provide any evidence that it addressed the leading practice.

Appendix III: Recommendations to Departments and Agencies

Department of Agriculture	To ensure the effective management of software licenses, we recommend that the Secretary of Agriculture take the following six actions:

- Develop an agency-wide comprehensive policy for the management of software licenses that addresses the weaknesses we identified.
- Employ a centralized software license management approach that is coordinated and integrated with key personnel for the majority of agency software license spending and/or enterprise-wide licenses.
- Establish a comprehensive inventory of software licenses using automated tools for the majority of agency software license spending and/or enterprise-wide licenses.
- Regularly track and maintain a comprehensive inventory of software licenses using automated tools and metrics.
- Analyze agency-wide software license data, such as costs, benefits, usage, and trending data, to identify opportunities to reduce costs and better inform investment decision making.
- Provide software license management training to appropriate agency personnel addressing contract terms and conditions, negotiations, laws and regulations, acquisition, security planning, and configuration management.

Department of Commerce	To ensure the effective management of software licenses, we recommend that the Secretary of Commerce take the following six actions:

- Develop an agency-wide comprehensive policy for the management of software licenses that addresses the weaknesses we identified.
- Employ a centralized software license management approach that is coordinated and integrated with key personnel for the majority of agency software license spending and/or enterprise-wide licenses.
- Establish a comprehensive inventory of software licenses using automated tools for the majority of agency software license spending and/or enterprise-wide licenses.
- Regularly track and maintain a comprehensive inventory of software licenses using automated tools and metrics.
- Analyze agency-wide software license data, such as costs, benefits, usage, and trending data, to identify opportunities to reduce costs and better inform investment decision making.
- Provide software license management training to appropriate agency personnel addressing contract terms and conditions, negotiations, laws and regulations, acquisition, security planning, and configuration management.

Department of Defense

To ensure the effective management of software licenses, we recommend that the Secretary of Defense take the following six actions:

- Develop an agency-wide comprehensive policy for the management of software licenses that addresses the weaknesses we identified.
- Employ a centralized software license management approach that is coordinated and integrated with key personnel for the majority of agency software license spending and/or enterprise-wide licenses.
- Establish a comprehensive inventory of software licenses using automated tools for the majority of agency software license spending and/or enterprise-wide licenses.
- Regularly track and maintain a comprehensive inventory of software licenses using automated tools and metrics.
- Analyze agency-wide software license data, such as costs, benefits, usage, and trending data, to identify opportunities to reduce costs and better inform investment decision making.
- Provide software license management training to appropriate agency personnel addressing contract terms and conditions, negotiations, laws and regulations, acquisition, security planning, and configuration management.

Department of Education

To ensure the effective management of software licenses, we recommend that the Secretary of Education take the following six actions:

- Develop an agency-wide comprehensive policy for the management of software licenses that addresses the weaknesses we identified.
- Employ a centralized software license management approach that is coordinated and integrated with key personnel for the majority of agency software license spending and/or enterprise-wide licenses.
- Establish a comprehensive inventory of software licenses using automated tools for the majority of agency software license spending and/or enterprise-wide licenses.
- Regularly track and maintain a comprehensive inventory of software licenses using automated tools and metrics.
- Analyze agency-wide software license data, such as costs, benefits, usage, and trending data, to identify opportunities to reduce costs and better inform investment decision making.
- Provide software license management training to appropriate agency personnel addressing contract terms and conditions, negotiations, laws and regulations, acquisition, security planning, and configuration management.

Department of Energy

To ensure the effective management of software licenses, we recommend that the Secretary of Energy take the following six actions:

- Develop an agency-wide comprehensive policy for the management of software licenses that addresses the weaknesses we identified.
- Employ a centralized software license management approach that is coordinated and integrated with key personnel for the majority of agency software license spending and/or enterprise-wide licenses.
- Establish a comprehensive inventory of software licenses using automated tools for the majority of agency software license spending and/or enterprise-wide licenses.
- Regularly track and maintain a comprehensive inventory of software licenses using automated tools and metrics.
- Analyze agency-wide software license data, such as costs, benefits, usage, and trending data, to identify opportunities to reduce costs and better inform investment decision making.
- Provide software license management training to appropriate agency personnel addressing contract terms and conditions, negotiations, laws and regulations, acquisition, security planning, and configuration management.

Department of Health and Human Services

To ensure the effective management of software licenses, we recommend that the Secretary of Health and Human Services take the following six actions:

- Develop an agency-wide comprehensive policy for the management of software licenses that addresses the weaknesses we identified.
- Employ a centralized software license management approach that is coordinated and integrated with key personnel for the majority of agency software license spending and/or enterprise-wide licenses.
- Establish a comprehensive inventory of software licenses using automated tools for the majority of agency software license spending and/or enterprise-wide licenses.
- Regularly track and maintain a comprehensive inventory of software licenses using automated tools and metrics.
- Analyze agency-wide software license data, such as costs, benefits, usage, and trending data, to identify opportunities to reduce costs and better inform investment decision making.
- Provide software license management training to appropriate agency personnel addressing contract terms and conditions, negotiations, laws and regulations, acquisition, security planning, and configuration management.

Department of Homeland Security

To ensure the effective management of software licenses, we recommend that the Secretary of Homeland Security take the following five actions:

- Employ a centralized software license management approach that is coordinated and integrated with key personnel for the majority of agency software license spending and/or enterprise-wide licenses.
- Establish a comprehensive inventory of software licenses using automated tools for the majority of agency software license spending and/or enterprise-wide licenses.
- Regularly track and maintain a comprehensive inventory of software licenses using automated tools and metrics.
- Analyze agency-wide software license data, such as costs, benefits, usage, and trending data, to identify opportunities to reduce costs and better inform investment decision making.
- Provide software license management training to appropriate agency personnel addressing contract terms and conditions, negotiations, laws and regulations, acquisition, security planning, and configuration management.

Department of Housing and Urban Development

To ensure the effective management of software licenses, we recommend that the Secretary of Housing and Urban Development take the following four actions:

- Develop an agency-wide comprehensive policy for the management of software licenses that addresses the weaknesses we identified.
- Regularly track and maintain a comprehensive inventory of software licenses using automated tools and metrics.
- Analyze agency-wide software license data, such as costs, benefits, usage, and trending data, to identify opportunities to reduce costs and better inform investment decision making.
- Provide software license management training to appropriate agency personnel addressing contract terms and conditions, negotiations, laws and regulations, acquisition, security planning, and configuration management.

Department of the Interior

To ensure the effective management of software licenses, we recommend that the Secretary of the Interior take the following six actions:

- Develop an agency-wide comprehensive policy for the management of software licenses that addresses the weaknesses we identified.

- Employ a centralized software license management approach that is coordinated and integrated with key personnel for the majority of agency software license spending and/or enterprise-wide licenses.
- Establish a comprehensive inventory of software licenses using automated tools for the majority of agency software license spending and/or enterprise-wide licenses.
- Regularly track and maintain a comprehensive inventory of software licenses using automated tools and metrics.
- Analyze agency-wide software license data, such as costs, benefits, usage, and trending data, to identify opportunities to reduce costs and better inform investment decision making.
- Provide software license management training to appropriate agency personnel addressing contract terms and conditions, negotiations, laws and regulations, acquisition, security planning, and configuration management.

Department of Justice

To ensure the effective management of software licenses, we recommend that the Attorney General take the following six actions:

- Develop an agency-wide comprehensive policy for the management of software licenses that addresses the weaknesses we identified.
- Employ a centralized software license management approach that is coordinated and integrated with key personnel for the majority of agency software license spending and/or enterprise-wide licenses.
- Establish a comprehensive inventory of software licenses using automated tools for the majority of agency software license spending and/or enterprise-wide licenses.
- Regularly track and maintain a comprehensive inventory of software licenses using automated tools and metrics.
- Analyze agency-wide software license data, such as costs, benefits, usage, and trending data, to identify opportunities to reduce costs and better inform investment decision making.
- Provide software license management training to appropriate agency personnel addressing contract terms and conditions, negotiations, laws and regulations, acquisition, security planning, and configuration management.

Department of Labor

To ensure the effective management of software licenses, we recommend that the Secretary of Labor take the following four actions:

- Establish a comprehensive inventory of software licenses using automated tools for the majority of agency software license spending and/or enterprise-wide licenses.

- Regularly track and maintain a comprehensive inventory of software licenses using automated tools and metrics.
- Analyze agency-wide software license data, such as costs, benefits, usage, and trending data, to identify opportunities to reduce costs and better inform investment decision making.
- Provide software license management training to appropriate agency personnel addressing contract terms and conditions, negotiations, laws and regulations, acquisition, security planning, and configuration management.

Department of State

To ensure the effective management of software licenses, we recommend that the Secretary of State take the following six actions:

- Develop an agency-wide comprehensive policy for the management of software licenses that addresses the weaknesses we identified.
- Employ a centralized software license management approach that is coordinated and integrated with key personnel for the majority of agency software license spending and/or enterprise-wide licenses.
- Establish a comprehensive inventory of software licenses using automated tools for the majority of agency software license spending and/or enterprise-wide licenses.
- Regularly track and maintain a comprehensive inventory of software licenses using automated tools and metrics.
- Analyze agency-wide software license data, such as costs, benefits, usage, and trending data, to identify opportunities to reduce costs and better inform investment decision making.
- Provide software license management training to appropriate agency personnel addressing contract terms and conditions, negotiations, laws and regulations, acquisition, security planning, and configuration management.

Department of Transportation

To ensure the effective management of software licenses, we recommend that the Secretary of Transportation take the following six actions:

- Develop an agency-wide comprehensive policy for the management of software licenses that addresses the weaknesses we identified.
- Employ a centralized software license management approach that is coordinated and integrated with key personnel for the majority of agency software license spending and/or enterprise-wide licenses.
- Establish a comprehensive inventory of software licenses using automated tools for the majority of agency software license spending and/or enterprise-wide licenses.

- Regularly track and maintain a comprehensive inventory of software licenses using automated tools and metrics.
- Analyze agency-wide software license data, such as costs, benefits, usage, and trending data, to identify opportunities to reduce costs and better inform investment decision making.
- Provide software license management training to appropriate agency personnel addressing contract terms and conditions, negotiations, laws and regulations, acquisition, security planning, and configuration management.

Department of the Treasury

To ensure the effective management of software licenses, we recommend that the Secretary of the Treasury take the following six actions:

- Develop an agency-wide comprehensive policy for the management of software licenses that addresses the weaknesses we identified.
- Employ a centralized software license management approach that is coordinated and integrated with key personnel for the majority of agency software license spending and/or enterprise-wide licenses.
- Establish a comprehensive inventory of software licenses using automated tools for the majority of agency software license spending and/or enterprise-wide licenses.
- Regularly track and maintain a comprehensive inventory of software licenses using automated tools and metrics.
- Analyze agency-wide software license data, such as costs, benefits, usage, and trending data, to identify opportunities to reduce costs and better inform investment decision making.
- Provide software license management training to appropriate agency personnel addressing contract terms and conditions, negotiations, laws and regulations, acquisition, security planning, and configuration management.

Department of Veterans Affairs

To ensure the effective management of software licenses, we recommend that the Secretary of Veterans Affairs take the following six actions:

- Develop an agency-wide comprehensive policy for the management of software licenses that addresses the weaknesses we identified.
- Employ a centralized software license management approach that is coordinated and integrated with key personnel for the majority of agency software license spending and/or enterprise-wide licenses.

- Establish a comprehensive inventory of software licenses using automated tools for the majority of agency software license spending and/or enterprise-wide licenses.
- Regularly track and maintain a comprehensive inventory of software licenses using automated tools and metrics.
- Analyze agency-wide software license data, such as costs, benefits, usage, and trending data, to identify opportunities to reduce costs and better inform investment decision making.
- Provide software license management training to appropriate agency personnel addressing contract terms and conditions, negotiations, laws and regulations, acquisition, security planning, and configuration management.

Environmental Protection Agency

To ensure the effective management of software licenses, we recommend that the Administrator of the Environmental Protection Agency take the following six actions:

- Develop an agency-wide comprehensive policy for the management of software licenses that addresses the weaknesses we identified.
- Employ a centralized software license management approach that is coordinated and integrated with key personnel for the majority of agency software license spending and/or enterprise-wide licenses.
- Establish a comprehensive inventory of software licenses using automated tools for the majority of agency software license spending and/or enterprise-wide licenses.
- Regularly track and maintain a comprehensive inventory of software licenses using automated tools and metrics.
- Analyze agency-wide software license data, such as costs, benefits, usage, and trending data, to identify opportunities to reduce costs and better inform investment decision making.
- Provide software license management training to appropriate agency personnel addressing contract terms and conditions, negotiations, laws and regulations, acquisition, security planning, and configuration management.

General Services Administration

To ensure the effective management of its software licenses, we recommend that the Administrator of General Services take the following five actions:

- Develop an agency-wide comprehensive policy for the management of software licenses that addresses the weaknesses we identified.

- Establish a comprehensive inventory of software licenses using automated tools for the majority of agency software license spending and/or enterprise-wide licenses.
- Regularly track and maintain a comprehensive inventory of software licenses using automated tools and metrics.
- Analyze agency-wide software license data, such as costs, benefits, usage, and trending data, to identify opportunities to reduce costs and better inform investment decision making.
- Provide software license management training to appropriate agency personnel addressing contract terms and conditions, negotiations, laws and regulations, acquisition, security planning, and configuration management.

National Aeronautics and Space Administration

To ensure the effective management of software licenses, we recommend that the Administrator of the National Aeronautics and Space Administration take the following six actions:

- Develop an agency-wide comprehensive policy for the management of software licenses that addresses the weaknesses identified.
- Employ a centralized software license management approach that is coordinated and integrated with key personnel for the majority of agency software license spending and/or enterprise-wide licenses.
- Establish a comprehensive inventory of software licenses using automated tools for the majority of agency software license spending and/or enterprise-wide licenses.
- Regularly track and maintain a comprehensive inventory of software licenses using automated tools and metrics.
- Analyze agency-wide software license data, such as costs, benefits, usage, and trending data, to identify opportunities to reduce costs and better inform investment decision making.
- Provide software license management training to appropriate agency personnel addressing contract terms and conditions, negotiations, laws and regulations, acquisition, security planning, and configuration management.

National Science Foundation

To ensure the effective management of software licenses, we recommend that the Director of the National Science Foundation take the following four actions:

- Develop an agency-wide comprehensive policy for the management of software licenses that addresses the weaknesses we identified.
- Regularly track and maintain a comprehensive inventory of software licenses using automated tools and metrics.

- Analyze agency-wide software license data, such as costs, benefits, usage, and trending data, to identify opportunities to reduce costs and better inform investment decision making.
- Provide software license management training to appropriate agency personnel addressing contract terms and conditions, negotiations, laws and regulations, acquisition, security planning, and configuration management.

Nuclear Regulatory Commission

To ensure the effective management of software licenses, we recommend that the Chairman of the Nuclear Regulatory Commission take the following six actions:

- Develop an agency-wide comprehensive policy for the management of software licenses that addresses the weaknesses we identified.
- Employ a centralized software license management approach that is coordinated and integrated with key personnel for the majority of agency software license spending and/or enterprise-wide licenses.
- Establish a comprehensive inventory of software licenses using automated tools for the majority of agency software license spending and/or enterprise-wide licenses.
- Regularly track and maintain a comprehensive inventory of software licenses using automated tools and metrics.
- Analyze agency-wide software license data, such as costs, benefits, usage, and trending data, to identify opportunities to reduce costs and better inform investment decision making.
- Provide software license management training to appropriate agency personnel addressing contract terms and conditions, negotiations, laws and regulations, acquisition, security planning, and configuration management.

Office of Personnel Management

To ensure the effective management of software licenses, we recommend that the Director of the Office of Personnel Management take the following six actions:

- Develop an agency-wide comprehensive policy for the management of software licenses that addresses the weaknesses we identified.
- Employ a centralized software license management approach that is coordinated and integrated with key personnel for the majority of agency software license spending and/or enterprise-wide licenses.
- Establish a comprehensive inventory of software licenses using automated tools for the majority of agency software license spending and/or enterprise-wide licenses.

- Regularly track and maintain a comprehensive inventory of software licenses using automated tools and metrics.
- Analyze agency-wide software license data, such as costs, benefits, usage, and trending data, to identify opportunities to reduce costs and better inform investment decision making.
- Provide software license management training to appropriate agency personnel addressing contract terms and conditions, negotiations, laws and regulations, acquisition, security planning, and configuration management.

Small Business Administration

To ensure the effective management of software licenses, we recommend that the Administrator of the Small Business Administration take the following six actions:

- Develop an agency-wide comprehensive policy for the management of software licenses that addresses the weaknesses we identified.
- Employ a centralized software license management approach that is coordinated and integrated with key personnel for the majority of agency software license spending and/or enterprise-wide licenses.
- Establish a comprehensive inventory of software licenses using automated tools for the majority of agency software license spending and/or enterprise-wide licenses.
- Regularly track and maintain a comprehensive inventory of software licenses using automated tools and metrics.
- Analyze agency-wide software license data, such as costs, benefits, usage, and trending data, to identify opportunities to reduce costs and better inform investment decision making.
- Provide software license management training to appropriate agency personnel addressing contract terms and conditions, negotiations, laws and regulations, acquisition, security planning, and configuration management.

Social Security Administration

To ensure the effective management of software licenses, we recommend that the Commissioner of the Social Security Administration take the following six actions:

- Develop an agency-wide comprehensive policy for the management of software licenses that addresses the weaknesses we identified.
- Employ a centralized software license management approach that is coordinated and integrated with key personnel for the majority of agency software license spending and/or enterprise-wide licenses.

- Establish a comprehensive inventory of software licenses using automated tools for the majority of agency software license spending and/or enterprise-wide licenses.
- Regularly track and maintain a comprehensive inventory of software licenses using automated tools and metrics.
- Analyze agency-wide departmental software license data, such as costs, benefits, usage, and trending data, to identify opportunities to reduce costs and better inform investment decision making.
- Provide software license management training to appropriate agency personnel addressing contract terms and conditions, negotiations, laws and regulations, acquisition, security planning, and configuration management.

U.S. Agency for International Development	To ensure the effective management of software licenses, we recommend that the Administrator of the U.S. Agency for International Development take the following five actions: - Develop an agency-wide comprehensive policy for the management of software licenses that addresses the weaknesses we identified. - Establish a comprehensive inventory of software licenses using automated tools for the majority of agency software license spending and/or enterprise-wide licenses. - Regularly track and maintain a comprehensive inventory of software licenses using automated tools and metrics. - Analyze agency-wide software license data, such as costs, benefits, usage, and trending data, to identify opportunities to reduce costs and better inform investment decision making. - Provide software license management training to appropriate agency personnel addressing contract terms and conditions, negotiations, laws and regulations, acquisition, security planning, and configuration management.

Appendix IV: Comments from the Department of Commerce

THE DEPUTY SECRETARY OF COMMERCE
Washington, D.C. 20230

April 30, 2014

Mr. Eric Winter
Assistant Director
Information Technology
Acquisition Management Issues
U.S. Government Accountability Office
Washington, DC 20548

Dear Mr. Winter:

Thank you for the opportunity to comment on the draft report from the U.S. Government Accountability Office (GAO) titled *FEDERAL SOFTWARE LICENSES: Better Management Needed to Achieve Significant Savings Governmentwide* (GAO-14-413).

We concur with the findings as they apply to the status of software license management within the Department of Commerce, and we partially concur with the recommendations made. We will

- develop an agency-wide comprehensive policy for the management of software licenses, and

- ensure that software license management training is provided to appropriate agency personnel.

Please contact Jerry Harper, Director of IT Policy and Planning, at 202-482-0222 if you have any questions.

Sincerely,

Patrick Gallagher
NIST Director performing the duties of the
Deputy Secretary

Appendix V: Comments from the Department of Defense

DEPARTMENT OF DEFENSE
6000 DEFENSE PENTAGON
WASHINGTON, D.C. 20301-6000

CHIEF INFORMATION OFFICER

Ms. Carol R. Cha   14 May 2014
Director
U.S. Government Accountability Office
Washington, DC 20548

Dear Ms. Cha:

    Attached is the Department of Defense (DoD) response to the GAO Draft Report, GAO Code -310998, "Federal Software Licenses: Better Management Needed To Achieve Significant Savings Governmentwide" dated April 16, 2014.

    If you have further questions please contact, Mr. Robert Smith at 571-372-4656, robert.j.smith84@mail.mil.

Sincerely,

Brian G. Wilczynski
Acting
DCIO, Information Enterprise

Attachments:
As stated

**GAO DRAFT REPORT DATED APRIL 16, 2014
GAO-14-413 (GAO CODE 310998)**

**"FEDERAL SOFTWARE LICENSES: BETTER
MANAGEMENT NEEDED TO ACHIEVE SIGNIFICANT
SAVINGS GOVERNMENTWIDE"**

**DEPARTMENT OF DEFENSE COMMENTS
TO THE GAO RECOMMENDATIONS**

RECOMMENDATION 1: To ensure the effective management of software licenses, GAO recommends that that the Secretary of Defense develop an agency wide comprehensive policy for the management of software licenses that addresses the weaknesses GAO identified.

DoD RESPONSE: Partially concur. DoD concurs that policy for the management of software licenses is necessary to address the weaknesses that GAO identified, however DoD does not concur that a centralized license management approach is appropriate for an agency of the size and complexity of the DoD. DoD will initiate a DoD plan for a software license reporting capability in accordance with FY14 NDAA requirements. This plan will include actions for developing appropriate license management policy that aligns with Federal Government-wide software license management policy and guidance to be issued by OMB as recommended by GAO in this report.

RECOMMENDATION 2: To ensure the effective management of software licenses, GAO recommends that that the Secretary of Defense employ a centralized software license management approach that is coordinated and integrated with key personnel for the majority of agency software license spending and/or enterprise wide licenses.

DoD RESPONSE: Partially concur. DoD concurs that the majority of agency software license spending and/or enterprise wide licenses should be managed using an approach that is coordinated and integrated with key personnel. DoD does not concur that a centralized license management approach is the most appropriate for an agency of the size and complexity of the DoD. As part of the FY14 NDAA Section 935 requirements, DoD plans to analyze alternatives to determine the most appropriate approach for software license reporting. Potential alternatives may include a centralized license management approach as well as decentralized approaches. The resulting plan will consider budget requirements required for implementing software license reporting capabilities.

RECOMMENDATION 3: To ensure the effective management of software licenses, GAO recommends that that the Secretary of Defense establish a comprehensive inventory of software licenses using automated tools for the majority of agency software license spending and/or enterprise wide licenses.

2

DoD RESPONSE: Partially concur. DoD concurs that inventory data should be collected for agency software licenses purchased and/or enterprise wide licenses. DoD does not concur that a comprehensive inventory for the majority of software regardless of dollar value is required. DoD intends to execute the requirements of the FY14 NDAA section 935 to plan for an inventory for all software licenses for which a military department spends more than $5 million annually on any individual title. Because the majority of existing software licenses owned by the agency are not maintained using automated tools today, it may be resource exhaustive to incorporate automated tools to establish inventories for the majority of agency software licenses and/or enterprise wide licenses. Furthermore, due to the decentralized nature of purchasing and license management today within DoD, it may not be practicable to retroactively collect standard data about historical license transactions.

RECOMMENDATION 4: To ensure the effective management of software licenses, GAO recommends that that the Secretary of Defense regularly track and maintain a comprehensive inventory of software licenses using automated tools and metrics.

DoD RESPONSE: Partially concur. DoD concurs that ensuring the effective management of software licenses requires regular tracking and maintaining software license inventory data for software using automated tools and metrics. However, maintaining comprehensive inventory data of all software titles regardless of spend may not be the appropriate solution for an organization the size and complexity of the DoD. DoD will analyze alternatives to determine the most appropriate approach for a software license reporting process to meet the FY14 NDAA Section 935 requirements. DoD intends to execute the requirements of the FY14 NDAA section 935 to plan for an inventory for all software licenses for which a military department spends more than $5 million annually on any individual title. Potential alternatives may include a centralized license management approach as well as decentralized approaches. The resulting plan will look at budget requirements required for implementing software license reporting capabilities.

RECOMMENDATION 5: To ensure the effective management of software licenses, GAO recommends that that the Secretary of Defense analyze agency wide software license data such as costs, benefits, usage, and trending data to identify opportunities to reduce costs and better inform investment decision making.

DoD RESPONSE: Concur. DoD CIO, in consultation with DoD Component CIOs, will analyze existing agency wide selected software license data that is being collected which meets the requirements of the FY13 NDAA, Section937. DoD will use the findings of this analysis to identify opportunities to reduce costs and inform decision-making about how to proceed with planning a department-wide license reporting capability.

3

RECOMMENDATION 6: To ensure the effective management of software licenses, GAO recommends that that the Secretary of Defense provide software license management training to appropriate agency personnel addressing contract terms and conditions, negotiations, laws and regulations, security planning, and configuration management.

DoD RESPONSE:
Concur. The DoD has established software license management training through the DoD Enterprise Software Initiative (ESI) that includes contract terms and conditions, negotiations, and laws and regulations. This training is available to DoD users who may be involved in asset management. DoD ESI will over time include additional topics related to software license and management best practices. The Defense Acquisition University provides training in security planning and configuration management. The plan for a software license reporting capability that DoD CIO will develop to address the requirements of Section 935 of the FY14 NDAA may identify needs for additional software license training.

Appendix: VI: Comments from the Department of Education

UNITED STATES DEPARTMENT OF EDUCATION

OFFICE OF THE CHIEF INFORMATION OFFICER

THE CHIEF INFORMATION OFFICER

May 1, 2014

Ms. Carol R. Cha
Director, Information Technology Acquisition Management Issues
Government Accountability Office
441 G Street, NW
Washington, DC 20548

Dear Ms. Cha:

I am writing to respond to recommendations made in the Government Accountability Office (GAO) draft report, "Federal Software Licenses: Better Management Needed to Achieve Significant Savings Governmentwide" (GAO-14-413). This report focused on the federal government's oversight of software license spending and management of software licenses that once implemented can result in significant cost savings. The U.S. Department of Education (Department) appreciates the opportunity to respond to the GAO report and the need to promote the use of best practices in software license management.

Since 2004, the Department has managed software licenses in a largely decentralized manner. This decentralized approach has limited the Department's ability to track software licenses, comprehensively inventory and easily determine which licenses were over- or under-purchased, and over- or underutilized. We believe the Department's new centralized approach to software license management incorporates the best practices identified in this GAO draft report. The Department is on track to implement a revised software acquisition policy in 2014, which will allow better management, tracking, and reporting of software licenses.

Our responses to GAO's specific recommendations to the Secretaries and Agency Heads of the 24 departments and agencies participating in the federal software license management initiative follow.

Recommendation 1: *Develop an agencywide comprehensive policy for the management of software licenses that addresses the weaknesses we identified.*

Response: The Department concurs with this recommendation. In response to the known weaknesses, we developed a Department-wide directive that establishes guidelines for software acquisition and management. The directive is in the final stages of review, and we expect approval by June 2014.

Recommendation 2: *Employ a centralized software license management approach that is coordinated and integrated with key personnel for the majority of agency software license spending and/or enterprisewide licenses.*

400 MARYLAND AVE. S.W., WASHINGTON, DC 20202
www.ed.gov

The Department of Education's mission is to promote student achievement and preparation for global competitiveness by fostering educational excellence and ensuring equal access.

Response: The Department concurs with this recommendation. The Department-wide directive currently in final review places central control for software license management within the office of the Chief Information Officer (CIO). The Office of the CIO will coordinate and integrate key personnel to ensure the majority of software licenses are managed in a manner consistent with the directive.

Recommendation 3: *Establish a comprehensive inventory of software licenses using automated tools for the majority of agency software license spending and/or enterprisewide licenses.*

Response: The Department concurs with this recommendation. Current tools provide an inventory of a significant portion of software licenses deployed by the Department. The Office of the CIO will identify and implement tools appropriate and necessary to support implementation of the directive addressing all software licenses by November 2014.

Recommendation 4: *Regularly track and maintain a comprehensive inventory of software licenses using automated tools and metrics.*

Response: The Department concurs with this recommendation. As noted above, the directive requiring the Department to regularly track and maintain a comprehensive inventory of software licenses using automated tools and metrics is in the final stages of review, and we expect approval of this directive by June 2014.

Recommendation 5: *Analyze agencywide software license data such as costs, benefits, usage, and trending data to identify opportunities to reduce costs and better inform investment decision making.*

Response: The Department concurs with this recommendation. As noted above, the directive requiring analysis of agency-wide software license data such as costs, benefits, usage, and trending data to identify opportunities to reduce costs and better inform investment decision making is in the final stages of review, and we expect to begin implementing this directive by June 2014.

Recommendation 6: *Provide software license management training to appropriate agency personnel addressing contract terms and conditions, negotiations, laws and regulations, acquisition, security planning, and configuration management.*

Response: The Department concurs with this recommendation. Upon final approval of the directive, we will provide training for the various roles identified in the process.

Again, I appreciate the opportunity to respond to the GAO report. If you or your staff members have any questions regarding our response, please contact Kenneth Moore at (202) 245-6908 or e-mail (ken.moore@ed.gov).

Sincerely,

Danny A. Harris, Ph.D.

Appendix VII: Comments from the Department of Energy

Department of Energy
Washington, DC 20585

May 1, 2014

Ms. Carol R. Cha
Director, Information Technology
Acquisition Management Issues
Government Accountability Office
Washington, DC 20458

Dear Ms. Cha:

Thank you for the opportunity to review the Government Accountability Office's (GAO) draft report, *Federal Software Licenses: Better Management Needed to Achieve Significant Savings Government-wide, GAO-14-413*. The Department of Energy's (DOE) Office of the Chief Information Officer (OCIO) has reviewed the draft report and the related recommendations. Our general comments are below and technical comments have been provided in an attachment.

The OCIO recognizes that the GAO was asked to review federal agencies' management of software licenses, specifically to: (1) assess the extent to which Office of Management and Budget (OMB) and federal agencies have appropriate policies on software license management; (2) determine the extent to which agencies are adequately managing licenses; and (3) describe agencies' most widely used software applications and the extent to which they were over or under purchased.

The DOE structure is comprised of semi-autonomous Administrations (NNSA, EIA, and Power Marketing Administrations) and Program Offices that manage contractor-operated facilities with diverse, highly specialized, and dynamic missions. Numerous Program, Operations, Site, and Functional Offices procure and manage separate IT services for DOE's approximately 15,000 Federal employees and direct support service contractors. As part of their operational responsibilities, the roughly 100,000 Laboratory, Plant, and Facility contractors also are charged with building effective and efficient IT programs to service their differing missions across the complex. As information technology continues to evolve, DOE's numerous Administrations and Program Offices must continually access functionality, to include software license requirements, to adapt and ensure that the technology continues to meet DOE operational responsibilities/mission requirements.

DOE makes great effort to coordinate and optimize the sharing of information technology solutions across its diverse components to efficiently and effectively meet business needs. The Department has taken a number of steps to aggregate licensing to achieve volume discounts, but at this time there are no plans to change Departmental policy to create a centralized software management program.

Printed with soy ink on recycled paper

The Department agrees that there may be opportunities to aggregate licensing to achieve volume discounts and integrate disparate but related data sources. The DOE IT Modernization Strategy, targeted for completion in FY16, (http://energy.gov/sites/prod/files/IT%20Modernization%20Strategy_0.pdf) seeks to reduce the number of product and service procurement vehicles and to leverage the collective buying power of DOE as well as to simplify and reduce the cost and complexity of Federal acquisitions. The Department will continue to encourage consolidation of software package acquisition and the use of volume purchasing arrangements through enterprise-wide agreements (EWA), and the application of best practices in software implementation. The EWA Program has proven effective in consolidating such acquisitions and providing cost savings. For example, our EWA to purchase Microsoft products saved an estimated $21 million over GSA pricing in the last five years and is relied upon to procure roughly 80% of Microsoft products in use by DOE and its Agencies.

Attached is the Department's response to the specific recommendations as well as clarifications of specific facts discussed in the draft report.

Thank you again for the opportunity to provide comments on this draft. We look forward to receiving your final report. If you have any questions related to this letter, please feel free to contact Ms. Sarah Gamage, Associate CIO for IT Corporate Management, at (301) 903-1059.

Sincerely,

Robert F. Brese
Chief Information Officer

Enclosure

Enclosure

<u>Response to Recommendations</u>

To ensure the effective management of software licenses, we recommend that the Secretary of Energy take the following six actions:

1. **Develop an agency-wide comprehensive policy for the management of software licenses that addresses the weaknesses identified;**

   DOE does have an agency-wide policy that addresses the management of software. DOE Order 200.1A encourages the "consolidation of software package acquisition, volume purchasing arrangements, enterprise wide agreements and best practices in software implementation", where appropriate.

2. **Employ a centralized software management approach that is coordinated and integrated with key personnel for the majority of agency software license spending and/or enterprise-wide licenses;**

   The OCIO's Enterprise Wide Agreement Program staff hosts periodic conference calls with key IT Representatives across the DOE complex. These individuals recommend common software for consideration by the EWA Program. Any software that has users in multiple locations can be considered for a centralized purchasing vehicle.

3. **Establish a comprehensive inventory of software licenses using automated tools for the majority of agency software license spending and or enterprise-wide licenses;**

   While the OCIO does not have a complete, current inventory of software licenses, we would argue that rather than 6% of the Department's footprint, the OCIO's tools and data collection information cover closer to 45% of the Federal space as it is defined in the Modernization Plan (15,000 Federal and direct support contractors). The Laboratories, Plants, and Facilities are considered separate for the purposes of the Commodity IT exercises. As with other exercises within PortfolioStat, the Department will implement future OMB guidance.

4. **Regularly track and maintain a comprehensive inventory of software licenses using automated tools and metrics;**

   As noted above, the services provided by the OCIO reach roughly 45% of the estimated 15,000 Federal employees and support service contractors in the Department. For that 45%, the OCIO does regularly track and maintain licenses and publishes the results on a monthly basis in the Energy IT Services Business Reporting System.

5. **Analyze agency-wide software license data such as costs, benefits, usage, and trending data to identify opportunities to reduce costs and better inform investment decision making; and**

Analysis is done on agency-wide software usage as part of the EWA Program's efforts. When a particular piece of software is identified as being in use at multiple locations, the CIO collects cost, benefit, usage, and trending data for that software. If it is determined to be cost effective to put an agreement in place, data continues to be collected as part of the contract vehicle.

6. **Provide software license management training to appropriate agency personnel addressing contract terms and conditions, negotiations, laws and regulations, acquisition, security planning, and configuration management.**

Training for Federal employees is managed on an office-by-office basis as part of the Individual Development and Training Needs Assessment Process. Individuals needing such training can be self-identified or identified by their supervisor for training.

Appendix: VIII: Comments from the Department of Health and Human Services

DEPARTMENT OF HEALTH & HUMAN SERVICES

OFFICE OF THE SECRETARY

Assistant Secretary for Legislation
Washington, DC 20201

MAY 6 – 2014

Carol R. Cha, Director
Information Technology Acquisition Management Issues
U.S. Government Accountability Office
441 G Street NW
Washington, DC 20548

Dear Ms. Cha:

Attached are comments on the U.S. Government Accountability Office's (GAO) report entitled, "Federal Software Licenses: Better Management Needed to Achieve Significant Savings Governmentwide" (GAO-14-413).

The Department appreciates the opportunity to review this report prior to publication.

Sincerely,

Jim R. Esquea
Assistant Secretary for Legislation

Attachment

**GENERAL COMMENTS OF THE DEPARTMENT OF HEALTH AND HUMAN
SERVICES (HHS) ON THE GOVERNMENT ACCOUNTABILITY OFFICE'S (GAO)
DRAFT REPORT ENTITLED, "FEDERAL SOFTWARE LICENSES: BETTER
MANAGEMENT NEEDED TO ACHIEVE SIGNIFICANT SAVINGS
GOVERNMENTWIDE" (GAO 14-413)**

The Department appreciates the opportunity to review and comment on this draft report.

The Department of Health and Human Services (HHS) previously responded to this GAO
inquiry on October 31, 2013. The submitted response addressed the need for HHS to further
instill governance with software license management and business processes at the Operational
Divisions (OpDIVs) and Headquarters level.

The Office of Chief Information Officer (OCIO) within HHS has implemented numerous best
practices and initiatives to promote cost savings and visibility regarding IT spending. Three of
the OCIO Top Priorities for FY2014 include the expansion of the Vendor Management Office
that is responsible for the establishment of enterprise license agreements and central management
of IT spending on software; facilitate an integrated data collection from all OPDIVs to retrieve
and analyze data regarding components of their infrastructure not limited to only software but
also regarding mobile and wireless contracts and network circuits; and, addressing PortfolioStat
segments to construct a department wide Cloud Services vehicle. Additionally, OCIO has
documented its enterprise wide visibility goals and strategies within the Business Intelligence
Roadmap, the Information Resource Management Plan as well as the implementation plan of the
Information Technology Steering Committee (ITSC). Each strategy is expected to provide
executive insight into IT spending and a foundation for successful enterprise wide cost savings
solutions across HHS.

1

Appendix IX: Comments from the Department of Homeland Security

U.S. Department of Homeland Security
Washington, DC 20528

May 14, 2014

Carol R. Cha
Director, Information Technology
Acquisition Management Issues
U.S. Government Accountability Office
441 G Street, NW
Washington, DC 20548

Re: Draft Report GAO-14-413, "FEDERAL SOFTWARE LICENSES: Better Management
Needed to Achieve Significant Savings Governmentwide"

Dear Ms. Cha:

Thank you for the opportunity to review and comment on this draft report. The U.S. Department of
Homeland Security (DHS) appreciates the U.S. Government Accountability Office's (GAO's) work
in planning and conducting its review and issuing this report.

The Department is pleased to note GAO's positive acknowledgement that DHS has identified
enterprise software licensing as a target area for cost savings or avoidance, and is fully
addressing all seven elements that a comprehensive software license policy should specify.
The DHS Enterprise License Agreements (ELAs) Program Office currently manages 10 ELAs
for the Department and maintains monthly cost avoidance reports of Component data that
reference product requirements, quantity, and pricing options. These cost avoidance reports
are used to identify opportunities to further reduce costs and better inform investment decision
making for enterprise software licensing.

The draft report contained five recommendations directed to DHS with which the Department
concurs. Specifically, GAO recommended that the Secretary of Homeland Security:

Recommendation 1: Employ a centralized software license management approach that is
coordinated and integrated with key personnel for the majority of agency software license
spending and/or enterprisewide licenses.

Response: Concur. The Under Secretary for Management (USM) directed the Office of the
Chief Information Officer (OCIO), the Office of the Chief Procurement Officer (OCPO), and
the Office of the Chief Financial Officer (OCFO) to work with key stakeholders to expand
upon its existing portfolio of centrally managed software. Additionally, the USM directed
OCIO, OCPO, and OCFO to develop an approach for the greater centralized management of
software licenses that will encompass the majority of the agency's software license spending.
Estimated Completion Date (ECD): March 31, 2015.

1

Recommendation 2: Establish a comprehensive inventory of software licenses using automated tools for the majority of agency software license spending and/or enterprise-wide licenses.

Response: Concur. The DHS OCFO, OCIO and, as applicable, OCPO will collaborate to establish a comprehensive inventory of high value software licenses and incorporate the inventory as part of the management approach to software licenses. The inventory will meet the expectations of leading practices for software licenses to include access to licensing information such as contract terms. ECD: January 31, 2015.

Recommendation 3: Regularly track and maintain a comprehensive inventory of software licenses using automated tools and metrics.

Response: Concur. DHS OCIO will track and maintain a comprehensive inventory of software licenses as part of our software license management approach. The tracking metrics will be related to employee usage and the number of licenses purchased, to ensure that costs are aligned with usage requirements in order to minimize unused licenses. ECD: January 31, 2015.

Recommendation 4: Analyze agency-wide software license data such as costs, benefits, usage, and trending data to identify opportunities to reduce costs and better inform investment decision making.

Response: Concur. The DHS OCIO, with support from the OCFO and OCPO, will continue to analyze the software license data collected across the Department, such as costs, benefits, usage, and trends, to help make better informed and cost-effective investment decisions. ECD: March 31, 2015.

Recommendation 5: Provide software license management training to appropriate agency personnel addressing contract terms and conditions, negotiations, laws and regulations, acquisition, security planning, and configuration management.

Response: Concur. DHS OCIO, in collaboration with the Office of the Chief Human Capital Officer and OCPO, will identify software license management training for appropriate personnel that includes software contract terms and conditions, as well as laws and regulations used for ELAs and software contracts. Additionally, the appropriate security, acquisition and configuration management policies and procedures will be outlined. ECD: December 31, 2014.

Again, thank you for the opportunity to review and comment on this draft report. Technical comments were provided separately. Please feel free to contact me if you have any questions. We look forward to working with you in the future.

Sincerely,

Jim H. Crumpacker, CIA, CFE
Director
Departmental GAO-OIG Liaison Office

2

Appendix X: Comments from the Department of Housing and Urban Development

U.S. DEPARTMENT OF HOUSING AND URBAN DEVELOPMENT
WASHINGTON, DC 20410-3000

CHIEF INFORMATION OFFICER

APR 2 9 2014

Ms. Carol R. Cha
Director, Information Technology
Acquisition Management Issues
U.S. Government Accountability Office
441 G Street, NW
Washington, DC 20548

Dear Ms. Cha:

Thank you for the opportunity to comment on the Government Accountability Office (GAO) draft report entitled, *FEDERAL SOFTWARE LICENSES: Better Management Needed to Achieve Significant Savings Governmentwide* (GAO-14-413).

The U.S. Department of Housing and Urban Development reviewed the draft report and has no comment. When the final report is released, the Department will provide a corrective action plan to address the recommendations for executive action.

If you have questions or require additional information, please contact Joyce M. Little, Chief, Audit Compliance Branch, at (202) 402-7404 (Joyce.M.Little@hud.gov) or Juanita L. Toatley, Audit Liaison, Audit Compliance Branch, at (202) 402-3555 (Juanita.L.Toatley@hud.gov).

Sincerely,

Kevin R. Cooke, Jr.
Acting Chief Information Officer

Appendix XI: Comments from the Department of the Interior

United States Department of the Interior

OFFICE OF THE SECRETARY
Washington, D.C. 20240

MAY 0 1 2014

Ms. Carol R. Cha
Director, Information Technology
Acquisition Management Issues
U.S. Government Accountability Office
441 G Street, N.W.
Washington, D.C. 20548

Dear Ms. Cha:

Thank you for the opportunity to review and comment on the Government Accountability Office (GAO) draft report entitled, *FEDERAL SOFTWARE LICENSES: Better Management Needed to Achieve Significant Savings Governmentwide* (GAO-14-413). We appreciate GAO's efforts to help guide agencies in managing software licenses.

The Department of the Interior (DOI) agrees with most of your findings and concurs with a majority of the recommendations and partially concurs with one recommendation. Please see a detailed response to each recommendation in the Enclosure.

If you have any questions about this response, please contact Lawrence Gross, Principal Deputy Chief Information Officer, at Lawrence_Gross@ios.doi.gov, or (202) 208-6194.

Sincerely,

Pamela Haze

Pamela Haze
Deputy Assistant Secretary for
Budget, Finance,
Performance and Acquisition

Enclosure

Enclosure

Department of the Interior
Comments on Draft GAO Report Entitled
FEDERAL SOFTWARE LICENSES: Better Management Needed to Achieve Significant
Savings Governmentwide (GAO-14-413)

Recommendation 1: Develop an agency-wide comprehensive policy for the management of software licenses that addresses the weaknesses we identified.

Management Comment: Concur. The Department of the Interior (DOI), Office of the Chief Information Officer (OCIO) will promulgate a comprehensive policy for centralized management of software licenses.

Recommendation 2: Employ a centralized software license management approach that is coordinated and integrated with key personnel for a majority of agency software license spending and/or enterprise-wide licenses.

Management Comment: Concur. The OCIO has received approval to hire a senior-level professional for vendor management. The OCIO in conjunction with the Office of Acquisition and Property Management (PAM) and the Interior Business Center (IBC) will have as a central function the responsibility for managing vendor services and strategic sourcing coordination relating to software and software licenses.

Recommendation 3: Establish a comprehensive inventory of software licenses using automated tools for the majority of agency software license spending and/or enterprise-wide licenses.

Management Comment: Concur. Several localized solutions have been implemented across DOI that include software license management capabilities (e.g. Service Now, Big-Fix, and BMC Remedy). The OCIO shall identify a standardized agency-wide solution to be centrally managed to address this finding.

Recommendation 4: Regularly track and maintain a comprehensive inventory of software licenses using automated tools and metrics.

Management Comment: Concur. The CIO shall identify a standardized, agency-wide solution to be centrally managed at the agency level to address this finding.

Recommendation 5: Analyze agency-wide software license data such as costs, benefits, usage, and trending data to identify opportunities to reduce costs and better inform investment decision making.

Management Comment: Concur. The OCIO in collaboration with PAM and IBC will conduct advanced analytics that will identify, on an agency-wide basis, software license data such as costs, utilization, and trending data to identify strategic sourcing opportunities to reduce costs and better inform investment decision making.

Recommendation 6: Provide software license management training to appropriate agency personnel addressing contract terms and conditions, negotiations, laws and regulations, acquisition, security planning, and configuration management.

Management Comment: Partially concur. DOI will continue to provide training on contract terms and conditions, negotiations, laws and regulations, as well as acquisition to appropriate contracting and Information Technology (IT) professionals on a regular recurring basis as a job prerequisite and as continued professional development. The training specified in the draft report is not unique to software licensing and is transportable between software licensing and other topic areas related to acquiring IT and other products and services. DOI does not agree that unique training is needed for software license management.

Appendix XII: Comments from the Department of State

United States Department of State
Comptroller
P.O. Box 150008
Charleston, SC 29415-5008

APR 3 0 2014

Dr. Loren Yager
Managing Director
International Affairs and Trade
Government Accountability Office
441 G Street, N.W.
Washington, D.C. 20548-0001

Dear Dr. Yager:

We appreciate the opportunity to review your draft report, "FEDERAL SOFTWARE LICENSES: Better Management Needed to Achieve Significant Savings Governmentwide" GAO Job Code 310998.

The enclosed Department of State comments are provided for incorporation with this letter as an appendix to the final report.

If you have any questions concerning this response, please contact Colleen Hinton, IT Manager, Bureau of Information Resource Management at (202) 634-0320.

Sincerely,

Christopher H. Flaggs, Acting

cc: GAO – Carol R. Cha
       IRM – Patricia Lacina
       State/OIG – Norman Brown

Department of State Comments to GAO Draft Report
FEDERAL SOFTWARE LICENSES: Better Management Needed to
Achieve Significant Savings Governmentwide
(GAO-14-413, GAO code 310998)

The Department of State welcomes the opportunity to comment on the draft report *Federal Software Licenses: Better Management Needed to Achieve Significant Savings Governmentwide.*

Recommendation 1: Develop an agency-wide comprehensive policy for the management of software licenses that addresses the weaknesses we identified.

Response: The Department of State (DOS) concurs with this recommendation and has identified policy changes as an action for the Enterprise License Action Committee (previously Steering Committee).

Recommendation 2: Employ a centralized software license management approach that is coordinated and integrated with key personnel for the majority of agency software license spending and/or enterprise-wide licenses.

Response: The Department of State concurs with this recommendation and has listed it as a topic of discussion for an Enterprise License Action Committee meeting.

Recommendation 3: Establish a comprehensive inventory of software licenses using automated tools for the majority of agency software license spending and/or enterprise-wide licenses.

Response: The Department of State concurs with this recommendation and is actively engaged with both the Department's IT operational directorate and procurement office to identify solutions.

Recommendation 4: Regularly track and maintain a comprehensive inventory of software licenses using automatic tools and metrics.

Response: The Department of State concurs with this recommendation and is actively engaged with the Department's IT operational directorate to identify solutions.

-2-

Recommendation 5: Analyze agency-wide software license data such as costs, benefits, usage, and trending data to identify opportunities to reduce costs and better inform investment decision making.

Response: The Department of State concurs with this recommendation and is actively engaged with both the Department's IT operational directorate and procurement office to identify solutions.

Recommendation 6: Provide software license management training to appropriate agency personnel addressing contract terms and conditions, negotiations, laws, regulations, acquisitions, security planning, and configuration management.

Response: The Department of State concurs with this recommendation and will bring it to the attention of the Enterprise Licensing Action Committee to identify what is already being done and the gaps that need to be identified.

Appendix XIII: Comments from the Department of the Treasury

DEPARTMENT OF THE TREASURY
WASHINGTON, D.C. 20220

APR 25 2014

Ms. Carol R. Cha
Director
Information Technology Acquisition Management Issues
U.S. Government Accountability Office
441 G Street, NW
Washington, DC 20548

Dear Ms. Cha,

Thank you for the opportunity to provide comments on GAO's Draft Report, *"Federal Software Licenses: Better Management Needed to Achieve Significant Savings Governmentwide (GAO-14-413)."* The Department of the Treasury has no comments on the Report and appreciates GAO's efforts in its development.

Please contact me at 202-622-1200 if you need anything further.

Sincerely,

Robyn East
Deputy Assistant Secretary for Information Systems
and Chief Information Officer

Appendix XIV: Comments from the Department of Veterans Affairs

DEPARTMENT OF VETERANS AFFAIRS
WASHINGTON DC 20420

May 6, 2014

Ms. Carol R. Cha
Acting Director, Information Technology
 Security Issues
U.S. Government Accountability Office
441 G Street, NW
Washington, DC 20548

Dear Ms. Cha:

The Department of Veterans Affairs (VA) has reviewed the Government Accountability Office's (GAO) draft report, *"FEDERAL SOFTWARE LICENSES: Better Management Needed to Achieve Significant Savings Governmentwide"* (GAO-14-413). VA generally agrees with GAO's conclusions and concurs with GAO's recommendations to the Department.

The enclosure specifically addresses GAO's recommendations and provides an action plan for each. VA appreciates the opportunity to comment on your draft report.

Sincerely,

Jose D. Riojas
Chief of Staff

Enclosure

Enclosure

Department of Veterans Affairs (VA) Comments to
Government Accountability Office (GAO) Draft Report
*"FEDERAL SOFTWARE LICENSES: Better Management Needed to Achieve
Significant Savings Governmentwide"*
(GAO-14-413)

<u>GAO Recommendation</u>: **To ensure the effective management of software
licenses, we recommend that the Secretary of Veterans Affairs take the following
six actions:**

<u>Recommendation 1</u>: **Develop an agencywide comprehensive policy for the
management of software licenses that addresses the weaknesses we identified.**

<u>VA Comment:</u> Concur. VA is currently developing a plan of action and milestones to
implement an agency-wide comprehensive policy. VA has a draft policy and expects to
finalize the comprehensive agency-wide policy within next 90-120 days.

<u>Recommendation 2</u>: **Employ a centralized software license management
approach that is coordinated and integrated with key personnel for the majority of
agency software license spending and/or enterprisewide licenses.**

<u>VA Comment:</u> Concur. As previously demonstrated to GAO as part of the fact finding
portion of this report preparation, VA established and staffed the Technology Innovation
Program (TIP) Office in late 2013. This office is coordinating efforts around centralized
software license management and has established a comprehensive SharePoint site
that lists major software enterprise license agreements and many key attributes. This
office will continue to work with key personnel to expand its scope until it has visibility
and oversight into all enterprise software licenses.

<u>Recommendation 3</u>: **Establish a comprehensive inventory of software licenses
using automated tools for the majority of agency software license spending
and/or enterprisewide licenses.**

<u>VA Comment:</u> Concur. VA has established an inventory in a central repository for
known software enterprise license agreements. The TIP Office is continuing to analyze
the data collected in an effort to establish meaningful and repeatable processes for
collection and usage of this data. VA is currently leveraging existing tools including but
not limited to Microsoft Systems Center Configuration Manager (SCCM), IBM Endpoint
Manager (IEM), and BMC Atrium Discovery and Dependency Mapping (ADDM), in
order to gain a better understanding of software asset installation footprint. In addition,
VA is considering implementing software normalization capabilities, usage data, and
integration of various software asset data elements necessary to support software asset
management decision-making processes.

Enclosure

Department of Veterans Affairs (VA) Comments to
Government Accountability Office (GAO) Draft Report
*"FEDERAL SOFTWARE LICENSES: Better Management Needed to Achieve
Significant Savings Governmentwide"*
(GAO-14-413)

<u>Recommendation 4</u>: **Regularly track and maintain a comprehensive inventory of
software licenses using automated tools and metrics.**

<u>VA Comment</u>: Concur. As stated in the response to recommendation 3, VA is
currently leveraging existing tools including but not limited to SCCM, IEM, and ADDM, in
order to gain a better understanding of software asset installation footprint. In addition,
VA is considering implementing software normalization capabilities, usage trend
analysis, and integration of various software asset data elements necessary to support
software asset management decision-making processes. This will enable VA to track
and maintain software licenses and metrics using automated tools.

<u>Recommendation 5</u>: **Analyze agencywide software license data such as costs,
benefits, usage, and trending data to identify opportunities to reduce costs and
better inform investment decision making.**

<u>VA Comment</u>: Concur. VA is currently implementing a structured and scheduled
approach to economic evaluation and requirements validation for the majority of
software enterprise license agreements. The TIP Office is creating repeatable
processes and templates that will facilitate rigorous evaluation and validation of known
software expenditures as well as a structured means under which all enterprise licenses
will be structured and operated. This recurring analysis will potentially identify cost
avoidance opportunities and aid future investment decision-making process.

<u>Recommendation 6</u>: **Provide software license management training to
appropriate agency personnel addressing contract terms and conditions,
negotiations, laws and regulations, acquisition, security planning, and
configuration management.**

<u>VA Comment</u>: Concur. Information Technology (IT) Resource Management/IT
Workforce Development (ITWD) will work with appropriate stakeholders to assess
detailed training needs in the area of software assessment management. ITWD will
acquire commercially available training for software asset management that complies
with international standards developed by the International Organization for
Standardization. ITWD will ensure the training is at the proper level and is delivered in
the most efficient modality to the identified target audience. Additionally, VA is in the
process of acquiring training for agency level subject matter experts in order to establish
a training curriculum that can be expanded to train individuals associated with software

2

Enclosure

Department of Veterans Affairs (VA) Comments to
Government Accountability Office (GAO) Draft Report
"FEDERAL SOFTWARE LICENSES: Better Management Needed to Achieve
Significant Savings Governmentwide"
(GAO-14-413)

license management. VA anticipates completion of curriculum recommendations and
providing that training to agency level staff by the end of 2014.

3

Appendix XV: Comments from the Environmental Protection Agency

UNITED STATES ENVIRONMENTAL PROTECTION AGENCY
WASHINGTON, D.C. 20460

MAY 1 5 2014

OFFICE OF
ENVIRONMENTAL INFORMATION

Mr. Eric Winter
Assistant Director
Information Technology Acquisition Management Issues
U.S. Government Accountability Office
Washington, DC 20548

Dear Mr. Winter:

Thank you for the opportunity to review and comment on GAO's draft report, "Federal Software Licenses: Better Management Needed to Achieve Significant Savings Government wide" (GAO-310998). The purpose of this letter is to provide the U.S. Environmental Protection Agency's (EPA) response to your assessments.

The draft report assesses EPA's practices for managing software licenses against six leading practices. The assessment finds EPA partially meeting two of the leading practices and not meeting four of the leading practices.

GAO Assessments:

Leading Practice	GAO Assessment
Develop comprehensive policy and procedures for management of software licenses	Partially meet
Centralize management of software licenses	Not meet
Establish a comprehensive inventory of software licenses	Partially met
Regularly track and maintain comprehensive inventories of software licenses using automated discovery and inventory tools and metrics	Not meet
Analyze the software license data to inform investment decisions and identify opportunities to reduce costs	Not met
Provide appropriate agency personnel with sufficient software license management training	Not met

EPA Response:

EPA partially agrees with GAO's assessment and acknowledges that there is work to be done in better managing software licenses for the agency. EPA has a strong foundation to build its software license management program, The agency currently offers training on the acquisition process, whether that be for software or other products and services. EPA centrally procures and manages enterprise-wide software licenses such as those used by all EPA employees such as Office 2013, Office365 (Exchange, Lync, SharePoint) or Adobe Connect. The agency's efforts to consolidate enterprise software procurements was the initial step in EPA's software license management approach.

EPA's enterprise software licenses management program will be based on identifying the most efficient and cost effective strategy which will be implemented in an incremental approach. Where appropriate, EPA will centralize software procurements of software where cost saving or other efficiencies can be realized.

In the coming months, EPA will begin assessing its existing automated tools, governance structures and other federal agencies processes and policies. Where possible, EPA will use existing automated tools to manage software licenses. EPA's software license management program's goal is to gain a comprehensive understanding of employees' software needs, visibility in the usage and procurement of software and to make informed procurement and maintenance decision to attain cost savings and efficiencies throughout the agency.

On behalf of the Environmental Protection Agency, thank you for the opportunity to review and comment on GAO's draft report. EPA is committed to and excited by the opportunity in developing a comprehensive, efficient and cost effective software license management program. If you have any questions, please contact Asfara Moghis at moghis.asfara@epa.gov.

Sincerely,

Harrell Watkins
Acting Director, Office of Technology Operations and Planning
 and Acting Chief Technology Officer

cc: EPA GAO Liaison Team
        Patricia Williams, OEI GAO Liaison
        Anne Mangiafico, Audit Coordinator
        Asfara Moghis, Senior Advisor

Appendix XVI: Comments from the General Services Administration

The Administrator

May 1, 2014

The Honorable Gene L. Dodaro
Comptroller General of the United States
U.S. Government Accountability Office
Washington, DC 20548

Dear Mr. Dodaro:

The U.S. General Services Administration (GSA) appreciates the opportunity to review and comment on the draft report, *Federal Software Licenses: Better Management Needed to Achieve Significant Savings Governmentwide*, (GAO-14-413). The U.S. Government Accountability Office (GAO) recommends that the GSA Administrator:

1. Develop an agency-wide comprehensive policy for the management of software licenses that addresses the weaknesses that were identified.
2. Establish a comprehensive inventory of software licenses using automated tools for the majority of agency software license spending and/or enterprise-wide licenses.
3. Regularly track and maintain a comprehensive inventory of software licenses using automated tools and metrics.
4. Analyze agency-wide software license data such as costs, benefits, usage, and trending data to identify opportunities to reduce costs and better inform investment decision making.
5. Provide software licenses management training to appropriate agency personnel addressing contract terms and conditions, negotiations, laws and regulations acquisition, security planning, and configuration management.

We agree with the findings and recommendations and will take appropriate action. If you have any questions or concerns, please do not hesitate to contact me at (202) 501-0800, or Ms. Lisa Austin, Associate Administrator, Office of Congressional and Intergovernmental Affairs, at (202) 501-0563.

Sincerely,

Dan Tangherlini
Administrator

cc: Carol R. Cha, Director, Information Technology Acquisition Management Issues, GAO

U.S. General Services Administration
1800 F Street, NW
Washington, DC 20405
Telephone (202) 501-0800
Fax (202) 219-1243

Appendix XVII: Comments from the National Aeronautics and Space Administration

National Aeronautics and Space Administration

Headquarters
Washington, DC 20546-0001

MAY 1 3 2014

Reply to Attn of: **Office of the Chief Information Officer**

Carol R. Cha
Director
Information Technology Acquisition Management Issues
United States Government Accountability Office
Washington, DC 20548

Dear Ms. Cha:

The National Aeronautics and Space Administration (NASA) appreciates the opportunity to review and comment on the Government Accountability Office (GAO) draft report entitled "Federal Software Licenses: Better Management Needed to Achieve Significant Savings Governmentwide" (GAO-14-413).

In the draft report, GAO addresses six recommendations to the NASA Administrator to ensure effective management of software licenses. GAO recommends that the NASA Administrator take the following action:

Recommendation 1: Develop an agencywide comprehensive policy for the management of software licenses that addresses the weaknesses identified.

Management's Response: Concur. NASA agrees. A comprehensive policy will be developed and provided to the appropriate personnel across the Agency, including senior management. Estimated completion dates: Complete policy document by October 1, 2014; complete training by December 1, 2014.

Recommendation 2: Employ a centralized software license management approach that is coordinated and integrated with key personnel for the majority of agency software license spending and/or enterprisewide licenses.

Management's Response: Partially concur. While the Enterprise License Management Team (ELMT) is a great mechanism for quite a few of the large enterprise license purchases, several of the large Information Technology (IT) contracts have purchasing of licenses embedded in the contract conditions. In several cases, NASA doesn't specify which software the contract requires but only specifies the service that is needed. This makes it difficult to employ one centralized software license management tool. Furthermore, porting (the process of adapting software so that an executable program can be created for a computing environment that is different from the one for which it was

2

originally designed) from the contractor's proprietary systems will be costly. In addition, the IT Security team is currently engaged in deploying enhanced capabilities of the NASA security scanning tool that could assist NASA in addressing software scanning deficiencies. To fully implement this recommendation will require several phases, working with NASA stakeholders to ensure both mission and institutional software is integrated. Estimated completion date: Dependent upon project funding to port contractor systems data to the ELMT system through a phased approach.

Recommendation 3: Establish a comprehensive inventory of software licenses using automated tools for the majority of agency software license spending and/or enterprisewide licenses.

Management's Response: Partially concur. To fully implement this recommendation will require changes to some of the large IT contracts at NASA to be able to automatically pull the licensing information into a centralized system, with increased costs. This will require process and resources that are not currently allocated. Estimated completion date: Dependent upon project funding to port contractor systems data to the ELMT system through a phased approach.

Recommendation 4: Regularly track and maintain a comprehensive inventory of software licenses using automated tools and metrics.

Management's Response: Partially concur. To fully implement this recommendation will require changes to some of the large IT contracts at NASA to be able to automatically pull the licensing information into a centralized system, with increased costs. This will require process and resources that are not currently allocated. Estimated completion date: Dependent upon project funding to port contractor systems data to the ELMT system through a phased approach.

Recommendation 5: Analyze agencywide software license data such as costs, benefits, usage, and trending data to identify opportunities to reduce costs and better inform investment decision making.

Management's Response: Concur. ELMT already does an excellent job of this kind of detailed analysis for the software under its purview. Better coordination with the large IT contracts and Center's software license management personnel and Agency acquisition personnel will be instituted. The Office of the Chief Information Officer (OCIO) will coordinate with the Headquarters Office of Procurement to increase awareness of NASA's Strategic Sourcing Initiatives that will incrementally reduce cost and inform various NASA stakeholders across the Agency of software consolidation opportunities that utilize ELMT and/or the IT Infrastructure Integration Program (I3P). Furthermore, the OCIO will request current consolidated contract services offices to report cost benefits the Agency has realized by leveraging Agency contracting vehicle that support NASA Strategic Sourcing Goals (e.g., Communication Service Office, End User Services, NASA Enterprise Apps Competency Center, Web Services, and Solutions for

3

Enterprise-Wide Procurement (SEWP). Estimated completion date: Analysis by
October 1, 2014.

Recommendation 6: Provide software license management training to appropriate
agency personnel addressing contract terms and conditions, negotiations, laws and
regulations, acquisition, security planning, and configuration management.

Management's Response: Concur. The NASA Shared Service Center (NSSC) located
at Stennis Space Center (SSC) in Mississippi will ensure that the ELMT will stay aware
of current trends, techniques, laws, and regulations associated with software license
management. In parallel, the ELMT will provide additional training to the Centers to
inform them of the advantages of leveraging the ELMT for software consolidated
purchases. Security planning and configuration management will remain in standard IT
Security training but will be reviewed for expansion of training to address the portion of
IT asset life-cycle management associated with deployment, maintenance, and retirement
that is specific to software life-cycle management. The ELMT will address the portion of
IT asset life-cycle management associated with requisition and procurement. Centers,
programs, and projects will remain responsible for Deployment, Maintenance, and
Retirement. Estimated completion dates: Additional ELMT training to Centers by
September 1, 2014; review of IT Security Training completed by
October 1, 2014.

Thank you for the opportunity to comment on this draft report. If you have any questions
or require additional information, please contact Ruth McWilliams at (202) 358-5125.

Sincerely,

Larry N. Sweet
Chief Information Officer

NATIONAL SCIENCE FOUNDATION
4201 WILSON BOULEVARD
ARLINGTON, VIRGINIA 22230

MAY 0 6 2014

Ms. Carol R. Cha
Director, Information Technology Acquisition Management Issues
U.S. Government Accountability Office
441 G Street, NW
Washington, DC 20548

Dear Ms. Cha:

Thank you for providing the opportunity to review the draft GAO Report "Federal Software Licenses: Better Management Needed to Achieve Significant Savings Governmentwide" (GAO 14-413). We have no comments on the draft report.

NSF is committed to continual improvement in information technology management, including our software license management practices. We appreciate GAO's interest and work in this area.

If you require any additional information, please feel free to contact me at anorthcutt@nsf.gov or (703) 292-8100.

Sincerely,

Amy Northcutt
Chief Information Officer

Appendix XIX: Comments from the Nuclear Regulatory Commission

UNITED STATES
NUCLEAR REGULATORY COMMISSION
WASHINGTON, D.C. 20555-0001

April 30, 2014

Mr. Eric Winter
Assistant Director, Information Technology
 Acquisition Management Issues
U.S. Government Accountability Office
Washington, DC 20548

Dear Mr. Winter:

Thank you for giving the U.S. Nuclear Regulatory Commission (NRC) the opportunity to review and comment on the U.S. Government Accountability Office's draft report GAO-14-413, "Federal Software Licenses: Better Management Needed to Achieve Significant Savings Governmentwide." The NRC has reviewed the draft report, is in general agreement with it, and does not have any comments.

Sincerely,

Mark A. Satorius
Executive Director
for Operations

Appendix XX: Comments from the Office of Management and Budget

EXECUTIVE OFFICE OF THE PRESIDENT
OFFICEOF MANAGEMENT AND BUDGET
WASHINGTON, D.C. 20503

May 19th, 2014

Ms. Carol R. Cha
Director
IT Acquisition Management Issues
Government Accountability Office
441 G Street, SW
Washington, DC 20548

Dear Ms. Cha:

Thank you for providing the Office of Management and Budget (OMB) the opportunity to review the draft of GAO's report on "Federal Software Licenses; Better Management Needed to Achieve Significant Savings Government-wide" (GAO-14-413) and the opportunity to provide comments on the draft report.

As an initial matter, we appreciate the time and energy that GAO has devoted to the review of agency performance with respect to software license management. Driving efficiency, especially in commodity IT is a tremendously important element of effectively managing IT. As the draft indicates, there are several management tools in place including:

- Executive Order 13589, **Promoting Efficient Spending**, which states, "Agencies should assess current device inventories and usage, and establish controls, to ensure that they are not paying for unused or underutilized information technology (IT) equipment, installed software, or services."
- M-12-10, **Implementing PortfolioStat** which states, "PortfolioStat will be a new tool that agencies use to assess the current maturity of their IT portfolio management process, make decisions on eliminating duplication, augment current CIO-led capital planning and investment control processes, and move to shared solutions in order to maximize the return on IT investments across the portfolio.
- M-13-02, **Improving Acquisition through Strategic Sourcing** which required, "a set of recommendations for management strategies for specific goods and services - including several IT commodities identified through the PortfolioStat process - that would ensure that the Federal government receives the most favorable offer possible."

We would submit some additional management tools in place that have significant bearing in this space that were not included in the draft report, including:

- M-04-08, **Maximizing Use of SmartBuy and Avoiding Duplication** of Agency Activities with the President's 24 E-Gov Initiatives, which directed agencies to, "Review all commercial software acquisitions for appropriateness for inclusion

into the SmartBuy program in order to leverage government purchasing power
and reduce redundant purchases."

- **Cross Agency Priority Goal: Cybersecurity**, which has a goal statement that
  reads, "Executive branch departments and agencies will achieve 95%
  implementation of the Administration's priority cybersecurity capabilities by the
  end of FY 2014. These capabilities include strong authentication, Trusted Internet
  Connections (TIC), and Continuous Monitoring."

We propose the report recognize these additional management policies are also being
leveraged to improve software licenses management. First, the SmartBuy memo both empowers
GSA to negotiate on the behalf of the executive branch and identifies very specific categories of
software that is to be applied therein. Specifically the memo includes:

1) AntiVirus
2) Database
3) Disaster Recovery
4) Document Imaging
5) Enterprise Resource Planning (Human Resource and Personnel Management,
   Finance Application)
6) Geospatial Information Systems
7) Network Management
8) Office Automation
9) Open Source
10) Statistical analysis

This memo along with PortfolioStat and Strategic Sourcing deliver a policy foundation
that allows us to leverage GSA and collaborate with agencies and monitor performance.

Additionally the Information Security Continuous Monitoring Mitigation element of the
Cross Agency Priority Goal and clarified in M-14-03, Enhancing the Security of Federal
Information and Information Systems, Software Asset Management (page 10) is a core focus of
Phase 1 in FY 2014.

While the goal of this draft report is concerned with the efficiency and utilization of
licensed software, the necessary first step in driving that efficiency is to have visibility into what
is to be managed. We submit that the effective management of installed software can serve more
than one goal. It can be used to understand the risk and vulnerabilities of the software that an
agency is using, and can also be used to support the acquisition of software within an agency.
Because of this requirement to better manage software, agencies now have the tools to identify
when there is underutilization of software and are better able to recapture those underutilized
licenses and deploy them to people who need them. Because of this policy agencies are better
equipped to tell the Senior Procurement Executive exactly how many licenses of a given
software product are deployed in the enterprise at any given time. This represents a new level of
reliability in the extent of an agency's requirement, and will greatly increase an agency's ability
to negotiate and deploy the software.

The review team may not have considered these two additional policy considerations in their initial assessment. But given these facts, we don't agree with the statement, "OMB and Federal Agencies Need to Improve Policies on Managing Software Licenses" on draft page 7 and concluding with the statement on draft page 9, "Until the agencies have sufficient direction from OMB, opportunities to systematically identify software license related cost savings across the federal government will likely continue to be missed."

Once again, we thank you for your effort to help us drive efficiency in federal agencies. We look forward to the final report and thank you for the opportunity to make comments.

Sincerely,

Steven VanRoekel
United States Chief Information Officer

Appendix XXI: Comments from the Office of Personnel Management

UNITED STATES OFFICE OF PERSONNEL MANAGEMENT
Washington, DC 20415

Chief Information
Officer

May 8, 2014

Ms. Carol R. Cha
Director, Information Technology
Acquisition Management Issues
U.S. Government Accountability Office
441 G Street, N.W.
Washington, DC 20548

Dear Ms. Cha:

We have reviewed your draft audit report GAO-14-413 "Federal Software Licenses Better Management Needed to Achieve Significant Savings Government-wide". We are in agreement with the findings and recommendations identified in the report and appreciate the input of the Government Accountability Office. As we continue to implement OPM's Strategic Information Technology (IT) Plan and develop a strong IT leadership and governance process, we will address the proper management, evaluation, measurement and monitoring of all IT investment decisions to include software licensing. Specific responses to your recommendations are provided below.

Responses to Recommendations:

1. Develop an agency-wide comprehensive policy for the management of software licenses.

As GAO correctly points out on page 50 of this report, OPM has already developed a comprehensive policy but has not yet implemented it in a comprehensive manner. First, as part of its incorporation of agile development practices in its Systems Development Life Cycle Policy, OPM will make any necessary adjustments consistent with the recommendations in this report. Second, as part of the consolidation of IT functions within CIO, we will develop a future Enterprise Architecture and governance process to identify investment priorities and invest wisely in both enterprise-wide software and infrastructure needs of OPM. As part of our IT governance structure, OPM will manage, evaluate, measure and monitor software investments to include the tracking, training and overall lifecycle management of its software assets.

2. Employ a centralized software license management approach.

As detailed in OPM's Strategic Information Technology (IT) Plan, we will centralize all IT functions within CIO to include all technology investments. This will ensure that, through the implementation of an effective enterprise architecture, we prioritize and invest in technology that achieves OPM's strategic mission. Specifically, investments in software licenses will be:

- Properly justified by a Business Case analysis that is accompanied by a Return on Investment analysis,

- Reviewed to ensure compatibility with the Enterprise Architecture, and

- Funded only if properly justified and approved under OPM's new governance process that will tie all investment decisions and priorities to the available funding sources.

3. Establish a comprehensive inventory of software licenses.

As part of its revision to the existing enterprise architecture and integration of all IT functions into CIO, OPM will develop a comprehensive inventory of software licenses and develop adequate controls over both the acquisition of new software investments and the potential decommissioning and disposal of existing software investments. This software inventory will be used as a baseline for decision-making to ensure compatibility and interoperability of all applications and systems at OPM.

4. Regularly track and maintain a comprehensive inventory of software licenses using automated tools and metrics.

As part of managing, evaluating, measuring and monitoring IT investments, OPM will strive to acquire the necessary automated tools (multiple tools for different platforms may be required) to manage the tracking of all of software items/modules in real time and to maintain compliance metrics with software publisher licensing requirements from acquisition through decommissioning and disposal.

5. Analyze agency-wide software license data to identify opportunities to reduce costs and better inform investment decision making.

As part of managing, evaluating, measuring and monitoring IT investments, OPM will analyze software license data to inform decision-making with regard to software maintenance renewals or replacement contract in light of the agency's architecture. This information will be presented to the Internal Review Board (IRB) for every software acquisition, including license renewals, in the context of meeting agency requirements. The IRB reviewers will look at the cost, benefit, dual usage, industrial strength quality, interoperability needs and alignment of the software selection to meet strategic and tactical goals at a lower total overall cost which benefits the agency.

6. Sufficient Training on Software License Management.

OPM will develop training guidance and instructions for software license management that includes topics for all systems administrators who are responsible for installing and configuring software publisher's products, as well as for program managers and project managers charged with oversight of projects requiring licensed software. The training and guidance will address recommendation-specific topics of training, such as contract terms and conditions, negotiations, laws, regulations and some other areas listed in the recommendation.

Sincerely,

Donna K. Seymour
Chief Information Officer

Appendix XXII: Comments from the Social Security Administration

SOCIAL SECURITY
Office of the Commissioner

May 02, 2014

Ms. Carol R. Cha
Director, Information Technology
Acquisition Management Issues
United States Government Accountability Office
441 G Street, NW
Washington, DC 20548

Dear Ms. Cha:

Thank you for the opportunity to review the draft report, "FEDERAL SOFTWARE LICENSES: Better Management Needed to Achieve Significant Savings Governmentwide" (GAO-14-413). We have enclosed our response to the audit report contents.

If you have any questions, please contact me at (410) 966-9014. Your staff may contact Gary S. Hatcher, our Senior Advisor for Records Management and Audit Liaison Staff, at (410) 965-0680.

Sincerely,

Katherine Thornton
Deputy Chief of Staff

Enclosure

**COMMENTS ON THE GOVERNMENT ACCOUNTABILITY OFFICE DRAFT
REPORT, "FEDERAL SOFTWARE LICENSES: BETTER MANAGEMENT NEEDED
TO ACHIEVE SIGNIFICANT SAVINGS GOVERNMENTWIDE" GAO-14-413**

Recommendation 1

Develop an agency-wide comprehensive policy for the management of software licenses that
addresses the weaknesses GAO identified.

Response

We agree. We have organized an Information Technology Asset Management (ITAM)
workgroup, which meets on a regular basis to plan, develop, and implement an ITAM strategy
and the associated agency policy. In addition, we implemented Hewlett Packard's (HP) Asset
Manager software to assist us with scanning, monitoring, and discovery activities which will
provide enterprise-level visibility and information about our asset inventory.

Recommendation 2

Employ a centralized software license management approach that is coordinated and integrated
with key personnel for the majority agency software license spending and/or enterprise-wide
licenses.

Response

We agree. We invest the bulk of our software licensing resources in mainframe software that
includes a centralized software license management process for the majority of our agency
software licenses. Our broader ITAM initiative mentioned above will focus on centralizing the
management of the remaining software licenses agency-wide.

Recommendation 3

Establish a comprehensive inventory of software licenses using automated tools for the majority
of agency software license spending and/or enterprise-wide licenses.

Response

We agree. We are exploring existing data sources that can inform our inventory/asset
management system and will consider adding other tools that help with controls. As indicated in
our response to recommendation one, we are implementing HP's Asset Manager, which, when
fully implemented, will help us manage our software inventory by tracking and reconciling our
license inventory, as well as our physical asset inventory. In addition, we are conducting a proof
of concept for a non-mainframe software discovery tool that integrates well with HP Asset
Manager. We also use a mainframe discovery tool that we plan to integrate with HP Asset
Manager later in fiscal year 2014.

Recommendation 4

Regularly track and maintain a comprehensive inventory of software licenses using automated tools and metrics.

Response

We agree. As mentioned in our response to recommendations one and three, the fully implemented HP's Asset Manager will be our tool to manage and track our software inventory. Also, the non-mainframe proof of concept tool and mainframe discovery tools will help us manage and track our software license management activities.

Recommendation 5

Analyze agency-wide departmental software license data such as costs, benefits, usage, and trending data to identify opportunities to reduce costs and better inform investment decision making.

Response

We agree. We currently do this manually on a contract-by-contract basis, with a focus on the highest-dollar contracts.

Recommendation 6

Provide software license management training to appropriate agency personnel addressing contract terms and conditions, negotiations, laws and regulations, acquisition, security planning, and configuration management.

Response

We agree. Internally, we will work with our systems, contracting, and training staff, to acquire the needed software license management training.

2

Appendix XXIII: Comments from the U.S. Agency for International Development

FROM THE AMERICAN PEOPLE

Carol R. Cha
Director, Information Technology Acquisition Management Issues
U.S. Government Accountability Office
Washington, DC 20548

Dear Ms. Cha:

I am pleased to provide USAID's formal response to the Government Accountability Office (GAO) draft report entitled "FEDERAL SOFTWARE LICENSES: Better Management Needed to Achieve Significant Saving Government-wide" (GAO-14-413).

This letter, together with the enclosed USAID comments, is provided for incorporation as an appendix to the final report.

Thank you for the opportunity to respond to the GAO draft report and for the courtesies extended by your staff in the conduct of this audit review.

Sincerely,

APR 2 8 2014

Angelique M. Crumbly
Assistant Administrator
Bureau for Management
U.S. Agency for International Development

Enclosure: a/s

USAID COMMENTS ON GAO DRAFT REPORT
No. GAO-14-413

To ensure the effective management of software licenses, GAO issued the following five recommendations:

Recommendation 1: We recommend that USAID develop an agency-wide comprehensive policy for the management of software licenses that addresses the weaknesses we identified.

USAID Response: We agree with this recommendation. USAID's Bureau for Management's Chief Information Officer (M/CIO) will develop an agency-wide comprehensive policy for the management of software licenses that addresses the five leading practices described in Table 24 of the GAO audit report (GAO-14-413) for which USAID is shown as either "partially met" or "not met".

Target Date: March 30, 2015

Recommendation 2: We recommend that USAID establish a comprehensive inventory of software licenses using automated tools for the majority of agency software license spending and/or enterprise wide licenses.

USAID Response: We agree with this recommendation. USAID's M/CIO will establish a comprehensive inventory of software licenses using automated tools for the majority of agency software license spending as determined by the amount of dollars identified for acquiring software licenses in the USAID budget submission for FY2014 or the quantity of enterprise wide licenses acquired with the oversight of M/CIO.

Target Date: March 30, 2015

Recommendation 3: We recommend that USAID regularly track and maintain a comprehensive inventory of software licenses using automated tools and metrics.

USAID Response: We agree with this recommendation. USAID's M/CIO will implement procedures to regularly track and maintain a comprehensive inventory of software licenses using automated tools and defined metrics.

Target Date: March 30, 2015

Recommendation 4: We recommend that USAID analyze agency-wide software license data such as costs, benefits, usage, and trending data to identify opportunities to reduce costs and better inform investment decision making.

2

USAID Response: We agree with this recommendation. USAID's M/CIO will implement procedures to analyze agency-wide software license data such as costs, benefits, usage and trending data and promulgate policies to use the results of such analysis to identify opportunities to reduce costs and better inform investment decision making.

Target Date: March 30, 2015

Recommendation 5: We recommend that USAID provide software license management training to appropriate agency personnel addressing contract terms and conditions, negotiations, laws and regulations, acquisitions, security planning, and configuration management.

USAID Response: USAID's M/CIO will implement a training program for software license management that includes coverage for contract terms and conditions, negotiations, laws and regulations, acquisitions, security planning and configuration management and provide the training to appropriate agency personnel.

Target Date: March 30, 2015

3

Appendix XXIV: GAO Contact and Staff Acknowledgments

GAO Contact	Carol R. Cha at (202) 512-4456 or ChaC@gao.gov
Staff Acknowledgments	In addition to the contact name above, the following staff also made key contributions to this report: Eric Winter, Assistant Director; Naba Barkakati; Virginia Chanley; Eric Costello; Rebecca Eyler; Dana Pon; and Niti Tandon.

GAO□s □ission	The Government Accountability Office, the audit, evaluation, and investigative arm of Congress, exists to support Congress in meeting its constitutional responsibilities and to help improve the performance and accountability of the federal government for the American people. GAO examines the use of public funds; evaluates federal programs and policies; and provides analyses, recommendations, and other assistance to help Congress make informed oversight, policy, and funding decisions. GAO□s commitment to good government is reflected in its core values of accountability, integrity, and reliability.
Obtaining Copies of GAO Reports and Testimony	The fastest and easiest way to obtain copies of GAO documents at no cost is through GAO□s website (http:□www.gao.gov). Each weekday afternoon, GAO posts on its website newly released reports, testimony, and correspondence. To have GAO e-mail you a list of newly posted products, go to http:□www.gao.gov and select □E-mail □pdates.□
Order by Phone	The price of each GAO publication reflects GAO□s actual cost of production and distribution and depends on the number of pages in the publication and whether the publication is printed in color or black and white. Pricing and ordering information is posted on GAO□s website, http:□www.gao.gov□ordering.htm.
	Place orders by calling (202) 512-6000, toll free (□66) □01-□0□□, or TDD (202) 512-25□□.
	Orders may be paid for using American Express, Discover Card, □asterCard, Visa, check, or money order. Call for additional information.
Connect with GAO	Connect with GAO on □acebook, □lickr, Twitter, and □ouTube. Subscribe to our RSS □eeds or E-mail □pdates. □isten to our Podcasts. Visit GAO on the web at www.gao.gov.
To Report □raud, Waste, and Abuse in □ederal Programs	Contact: Website: http:□www.gao.gov□fraudnet□fraudnet.htm E-mail: fraudnet@gao.gov Automated answering system: (□00) 424-5454 or (202) 512-□4□0
Congressional Relations	□atherine Siggerud, □anaging Director, siggerudk@gao.gov, (202) 512-4400, □.S. Government Accountability Office, 441 G Street NW, Room □125, Washington, DC 2054□
Public Affairs	Chuck □oung, □anaging Director, youngc1@gao.gov, (202) 512-4□00 □.S. Government Accountability Office, 441 G Street NW, Room □14□ Washington, DC 2054□

www.ingramcontent.com/pod-product-compliance
Lightning Source LLC
Chambersburg PA
CBHW080427060326
40689CB00019B/4403